Lucky Genes

LUCKY GENES

by

DR JEAN WATKINS

[handwritten inscription: Margaret, with all best wishes Dr Jean Watkins (J. Watkins)]

The Memoir Club

© Jean Watkins 2010

First published in 2010 by
The Memoir Club
Arya House
Langley Park
Durham
DH7 9XE
Tel: 0191 373 5660
Email: memoirclub@msn.com

British Library Cataloguing in
Publication Data.
A catalogue record for this book
is available from the
British Library

ISBN: 978-1-84104-500-9

Typeset by TW Typesetting, Plymouth, Devon
Printed by J F Print, Sparkford, Somerset

To my grandfather, George Watkins,
who must have first inspired me with the
memories of his Round the World trip in 1934,
and of whom I was particularly fond.

Contents

List of Illustrations

Acknowledgements

Grateful thanks are due to my family who have contributed so many ideas and supported me throughout the writing of the book, to my friend Heather Cowell-Parker who has patiently and painstakingly proofread my script, and to Mike Edwards who took my picture for the cover. It's very rarely that I allow myself to be photographed, I prefer to be behind the camera, taking others!

Foreword

Friendships are forged along life's journey and it has been my good fortune to make Jean's acquaintance, although sadly not until recent times. This is obviously my loss as *Lucky Genes* is a well-researched, thought-provoking and entertaining memoir which recounts so many fascinating life-changing events which have fashioned the delightful personality of Jean as I know her today.

My first encounter with her was at a meeting of the Bournemouth and Poole Medical Society and it was not long before we found ourselves working together in the roles of President with Jean as President-elect, and during my year of office she gave me unfailing support and encouragement. Then Jean as President brought her calm approach and honed organizational skills to compile the season's programme of interesting talks drawing on her many personal contacts and experiences. But it was at the traditional President's end-of-term party held in the delightful Abbotsbury Tropical Gardens that Jean's impish sense of humour surfaced, for after we had been wined and dined we were entreated to take part in a brain-teasing quiz – and no one demurred! We should have expected such as we read in her book that on holiday traditional games run through the Watkins family and it is a delight to receive full instructions in this memoir about several exciting new ones and 'Racing Demon' and 'Up Jenkins' have been added to my list of family favourites for future after-supper entertainment.

Putting pen to paper to write an autobiography provides an opportunity for retrospection and inevitably with the passage of time there can be a loving appreciation of family and friends and especially of those who have nurtured us when young and provided our first opportunities to shine. In Jean's case we soon realise that it was her father who steered her into medicine for which she, and I would surmise countless patients, should be grateful for the skill and kindness imparted by this dedicated practitioner.

Her grandfather, George Watkins, merits the book's dedication 'as he inspired me with the memories of his Round the World Trip in 1934' and there can be no doubt that he transferred his love of travel to his granddaughter.

We discovered early on in our friendship that we shared the excitement and thrill of visiting countries not on the usual tourist trail. However my first visit to China in1989 paled into insignificance when I discovered Jean had embarked on a medical journey to China in 1978 and it was this tour which prompted her to purchase her first camera and to write articles for publication, as her adventures took her to seek tigers in Nepal, explore deep into Cambodia and Vietnam to mention only a couple of places to capture the author's attention. With such a record I could well envisage Jean signing up for a lunar trip as soon as it becomes a practical possibility.

In just over 100 pages of this well-written and illustrated memoir it is easy to have empathy with this story of a woman's life which reflects the joys, frustrations, disappointments, sheer hard work and dedication of a professional and personal life well spent and obviously with plenty more to come.

'Am I the person I am today because of my inherited genes or have the experiences that I have lived through been the bigger influence on my life?' challenges the author.

You will have to read this memoir to decide your response. In doing so you are in for a treat: enjoy.

Dame Margaret Seward DBE CBE

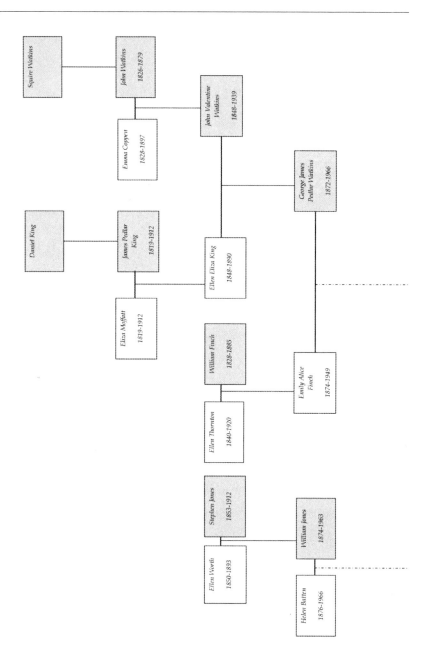

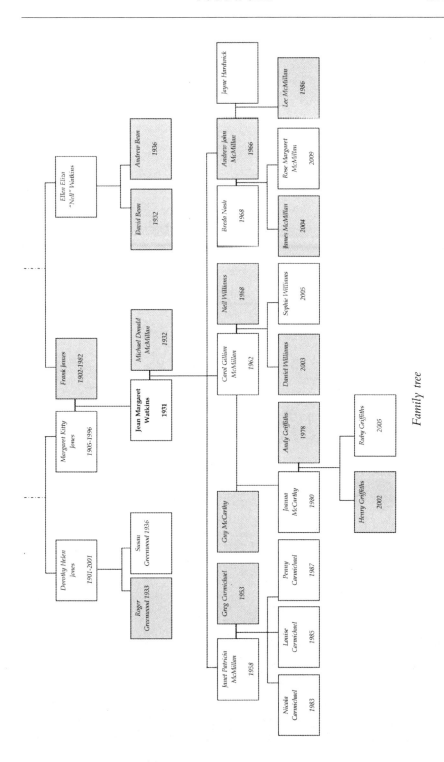

Family tree

CHAPTER 1

The great arrival (1931)

O N 9 OCTOBER 1931 – AT 1.30 A.M., my life began. As first born to a loving family there was great rejoicing, not only for my parents, but also my four, still surviving grandparents. I understand that the birth was a difficult one. Today, it would have been a hospital delivery, but in those days home deliveries were the norm, the forceps were produced and the doctor and the nurse just got on with the job in hand and my entry to the world was achieved. The 8 ½ lb bundle of joy faced an unknown future.

The venue was 7 Fern Villas, Barmouth, North Wales, far from my parents' home near the River Thames at Greenwich. Life for them had not been easy since their marriage two years before. It was the time of the Great Depression, heralded by the Stock Exchange Crash in New York in 1929. My father, a qualified Civil Engineer was employed by the Demolition and Construction Company. With things deteriorating, in 1930 he was threatened to become one of the 20 per cent unemployed in the UK. A letter arrived informing him that the company could no longer afford to pay his salary. Not one to give up under pressure, he continued to turn up at the office and work for nothing. Such obstinacy obviously paid dividends and it was with great pride that, many years later, he received a second letter appointing him to act as a Director on the Board of the firm.

Home life must have been tight in those meagre times. Once married, they had temporarily moved into a flat while awaiting completion of the new home that my grandparents had generously given them as a wedding present. The great day came, the move took place and all was ready at 99 Canberra Road, Charlton, SE7. My father returned that day from the office – with news! He had been offered a job, with pay, but the job was all those miles away in North Wales. Unemployment in the country was such that the offer could not be refused. The dream home had to be left and they settled in the flat at Barmouth, to work on the new promenade there, as well as to await my arrival.

Needless to say, I have no memory of the great event of birth, indeed, we returned to London when I was three months old. The only additions to my later learned vocabulary were *noswaith dal* (good morning) and *bora dal* (good evening).

Since that time I have returned twice to Barmouth. Once, just before the Second World War, in the summer of 1939. We stayed on the front at the Miramar Hotel, visited the old haunts, my birthplace and some of the beautiful surrounding areas. One memorable trip was to the top of Snowdon in the famous Snowdon Mountain Railway. First opened in 1896, it was built on the rack and pinion system learned from the Swiss. We travelled to the top (3,569 ft) in the old type carriages, open to the elements above waist level, with the only protection of flimsy canvas curtains. Luckily for us the weather was perfect. Today's transport, I understand, has been upgraded with windows, to protect passengers from the often inclement weather. The main memory of our other adventure was the attempt to climb a different mountain – Cader Idris. We did not make it to the top, but one day I must go back and try to rescue the tooth that I managed to shed half way up. Who knows, the tooth fairy may have found it and left a reward!

My second return was seventy years later in 2009. The beauty of the Snowdonia National Park revealed itself once more as we drove back towards my birthplace, where, with Andrew, my son, and his young family we really appreciated the magnificent two miles of sandy beach and rock pools that lay along the shores of Barmouth Harbour. At low tide, it seemed to stretch on forever. The beach is still separated from the town by the sea wall. Some of this is original from the days of 1931 when my father was involved in the building of, what was said to be, an 'excellent promenade'. However, there seems to be general disapproval of the later changes involved in creating a 'sea return wall to provide greater sea defence'. Around 1970 it was deemed necessary to protect the land, as well as unwary tourists, from the ravages of the tidal race that scoured a deep channel between the mainland and the island of sand dunes. To quote from Barmouth information on the internet, it is said that the new sea wall 'diminished the aesthetic and amenity value' of my father's work.

Tourism first became popular in Barmouth after the building of the railway in 1867. Subsequent escalation in the numbers of visitors does not seem to have improved the place. Now, no longer the busy trading port for the shipping out of herrings, wool and slate, the centre around the railway station is blessed with candyfloss stalls, fun rides for children and tourist shops offering an army of buckets, spades, lilos and an endless choice of tatty goods.

However, as well as the beach experience, my visit was not wasted as I learned more about 'our promenade'. During its construction, they hit upon a 'large block of stone 6 feet by 3 feet and about 9 inches thick'. It lay buried 20 feet below the high-water mark. Historians decided that this was 'the other stone' said to have been mentioned by a Lewis Morris in 1737, a so-called archaeological find. My father's heart must have sunk while work was delayed, the stone examined and retrieved and eventually taken to its final resting place in a local church nearby. The work was later completed and I learned that some important person was invited to officiate at its opening. Perhaps I was there too!

CHAPTER 2

My Watkins ancestors
(nineteenth century to 1920s)

THE RESEARCH OF FAMILY TREES is now a popular pursuit of many. What is the fascination with the past and the pressing need to know our roots? Personally, I have not pursued the research to its limit, but have been fortunate enough to hold some of the papers and letters of some of my forbears and in particular those that were handed on to me by my paternal grandfather, namely George James Pedlar Watkins (my Grandpa Watkins). The earliest records take us back to the year of 1794. Daniel King was applying to the Admiralty, on his retirement, for a reasonable pension. It is written in copybook handwriting and I can only suppose that he acquired a scribe to pen it, unless, by some miracle he had received sufficient education to be literate. It would seem that redundancy was still a factor even 150 years ago. The letter reads as follows:

Statement of the Services of Daniel King, Master of the Ant Hoy Belonging to Deptford.

May it please your Lordships –

That a reduction of Hoys is to take place, and as I have in consequence of my age and length of service been selected to be pensioned, I honestly beg leave to take this opportunity to lay my services before your Lordships – I entered the Royal Navy in the Orion 74 Guns, Captain Thomas Duckworth and was engaged as Powder Boy in the action off Ushant on the 28th and 29th of May and 1st June 1794. In 1795 I followed Captain Duckworth into the Leviathen and besides assisting at the capture of a large number of enemy's vessels, I was present at the unsuccessful attack on Levjane, St Domingo, and having joined the 'Africa' (in consequence of an attack of Yellow Fever) for passage home in April 1796, was paid off that year. I then apprenticed myself to the master of a Collier, and was after serving my time pressed, and sent on board the 'Vesuvius' 13th August 1808 under Captains Cunningham, and Saunders during which serving I was present at the bombardment of Flushing. I was then drafted into the 'Gorgon' and served under Captains Webb, Milner, de Crespigny and Bowden as A.B and Coxswain, afterwards in the Alcmere as Coxswain until 2nd December 1815 under Captain Jeremiah Coghlan when I was laid off. I was then employed in the Merchant Service until July 1832, when I was entered as mate in the Hoy service and served until February 1830, when I was made Master and have since that date piloted many of her Majesty's Ships and vessels down the river; and up to the present time have done my best to give satisfaction to my superiors. I therefore earnestly pray in consideration of the length and nature of my services, your Lordships will be pleased to grant me a pension that will enable me to procure some of the comforts necessary to my declining years. And I shall as ever bound pray.

One presumes that by the time he made this plea to the Admiralty in 1857 that he must have been getting on in years, certainly in his sixties. Surely, he must have been very young when he began his career as a powder boy, or powder monkey as they were called in those days. We have no knowledge of any antecedents so it may be possible that he was either orphaned, sold into the Navy or had run away from home.

A visit to the *Victory* at Portsmouth, drove home to me the appalling conditions, treatment and dangers that he must have endured in those early days. We were told that the boys were taken on from the age of eleven and entered the ship by way of the narrow steps on the outside of the boat, as far as the upper deck. After a preliminary training, that might have included the chance to read and write, he would be signed on, allotted a hammock and put to work. His duties were to attend to the men in a variety of menial ways, scrub the decks, clean out the toilets and the mangers where animals were kept, and when in battle, keep the guns supplied with gunpowder, whilst also dousing it down to prevent explosions. For his pains he might receive the princely sum of £7 or £8 a year, plus his board. Meals do not sound particularly exciting either. Breakfast might include cold porridge, ships biscuits, often alive with weevils, cocoa or coffee. Lunch might provide salt beef or fish with dried peas, rice or oatmeal, while at supper they might be back to the weevil-infested biscuits, worm-infested cheese and rancid butter. Drinks would be laced with lemon juice to prevent scurvy and although an allowance of rum, beer or wine was issued, drunkenness was not tolerated.

The day started early and there must be immediate response to the early morning call. If they were not quick enough to leave their hammock, the boatswain would come along and hit them with a tarred rope (called a starter), to get them moving. Should punishment be required, for any reason, all were summoned to the quarter deck to witness a flogging with the cat-o'-nine tails, after which the victim would be taken down to the ship's surgeon to have salt, the cheapest antiseptic, rubbed in to the wounds. Medicines were not free and would have to be paid for out of their meagre earnings. No doubt, the life of a pressed worker on ship was no picnic either.

Of home life, if any, we have no records but it does appear from later correspondence that he married and had a daughter and a son, James Pedlar King (1819–1912).

We do not know the response of the Admiralty to his plea dated 10 March 1857; but there is the following from an A.J.A. Cape Supe, stating that it had been, 'Submitted and I beg to observe that the conduct and ability of this Master, induce me to recommend him for the most favourable consideration their Lordships may be pleased to recommend him'.

However, there is further correspondence which suggests that Daniel King was not entirely satisfied with the result. It is dated May 1858 and reads as follows:

To the right Honourable the Lords Commisioners of the Admiralty
   My Lords
   I beg most respectfully to represent to you the circumstances of distress into which I am unexpectedly thrown on account of the loss of a Library Case said to have been shipped on board the Ant Hoy at Thurneys Victualling Depot on the 8th December 1854 for Deptford. – Immediately on my arrival at Deptford I was partly unloaded, when I was required to take on board a large number of packages (chiefly private) for AM Ships in the Mediterranean shipment in this 'Cottingbury' Transport lying off Deptford, it is therefore very possible that from the packages being similar to the Library Case it was shipped on board this vessel in mistake, and I beg to state to your Lordships that altho' it is stated I signed a receipt for the case in question yet in this hurry of loading and leaving it was impossible for

me to have taken into account of the stores that came into my vessel. And at this distance of time cannot state with certainty that this case was actually received by me especially as its arrival at Deptford was not in doubt until 4 or 5 months afterwards.

The payment of £79 2s. 8d. for this case having been demanded from me by the Accountants Generals letter of the 23rd April last. I beg most respectfully to remind your Lordships of my depressed circumstances, being entirely dependent of myself and an afflicted wife and daughter on my superannuation which is at the rate of two shillings and sixpence per day after 45 years of servitude with an unblemished character.

Your lordships will therefore perceive that it is impossible for me to meet this demand in my depressed condition which it is earnestly hoped my long and creditable services will induce your Lordships to forego a mark of compassion which will be most gratefully acknowledged by

My Lords

Your most obedient and humble servant

Daniel King Late Master of the Ant Victually Yard 33, Albert Str, Deptford.

Sadly we have no records about the outcome of the case.

His son James appears to have inherited the adventuring spirit and with others was involved in a battle on the Nile; he, himself, set off on an expedition to the Arctic in search of Franklin. He also maintained his contact with the sea in a marriage to an Elizabeth Moffat whose brother was a sea captain. Both lived to the ripe old age of ninety-three, dying within twenty-four hours of each other in 1912. They produced a daughter, Eliza Elizabeth King (1848–90). She introduced the name of Watkins to the family when she married my great-great-grandfather John Valentine Watkins (1848–1939), a man who hailed from eminent stock, with a grandfather by the name of Squire Watkins from Westerham in Kent, where he was said to be a landowner.

Life is very much a game of chance and the rest of the story could have been so very different if my great-grandfather had followed his initial inclinations. At the age of nineteen, John Valentine Watkins took the step of leaving home, with his uncle, Hugh Watkins. Hugh travelled with his wife, Martha, and their young son Hugh Daniel. They travelled on a ship called the *Netherby,* one of the Black Ball liners that had made three previously similar trips, for those wishing to emigrate to Australia, at the cost of £28. Gone were the days of convict deportation, but land and the lure of gold was attracting people to this far-off land in the 1860s. I am presuming that they boarded the ship at the London Docks on 1 April 1876 with 413 passengers, before collecting more at Plymouth. Finally, they left the shores of home and set sail for Queensland on 13 April. We have been lucky enough to trace a copy of a fully descriptive letter that was written by a sixteen-year-old boy on the journey, to his mother in England, reassuring her that he was all right and graphically detailing the adventures they had had on the way. Other reports that have come to light are those of the Superintendent Surgeon, and various newspaper articles written at the time of the shipwreck.

It seems that most of the journey was relatively uneventful but rather 'slow and tedious', with 'light wind and calm' all the way to the Cape of Good Hope. After this they were trapped below deck, cold and 'without fresh air or daylight', for two weeks, while the gales blew and the sea raged, and apparently washed away anything on deck that was moveable. The Superintendent Surgeon was kept busy with those suffering with 'coughs, colds and diarrhoea', two births and also the death of two infants that were said to have been sickly when they initially boarded the vessel. He reported the behaviour of the married couples to be excellent but that 'the single men were sometimes very outrageous in their behaviour'. Whether my great-grandfather was included amongst these I know not! If he was one of the sinners, he would have been brought under control by being put in irons, and having his rations stopped for a week at a time. However, one can imagine the problems that might arise on this small ship, especially at times when they were cooped up for days on end, in cramped quarters, and with the additional exuberance of 100 children under the age of twelve. Food and water were said to be good, apart from the flour that remained lumpy and sour for the whole journey.

By 13 July, after three months at sea, the weather changed and became very foggy with heavy rain at times. The Captain was having difficulty in determining his exact position. Nevertheless he decided to continue his course through the Bass Strait. This was his big mistake; on the evening of 14 July, 'the ship struck a reef on the west side of King's Island'. Panic struck as many 'rushed on deck groaning and praying – some who had never prayed before'. Land was within sight, just 200 yards away, but the heavy breakers on the shore were too much for any attempt to land a boat that night. All night the vessel 'groaned and creaked as if she would go over altogether at every roll'. With a great hole in the side of the ship, she was full of water and, had they not been stuck on the rocks she would have quickly sunk. The one thing that was rescued from the holds was rum, whisky and tobacco which ensured that most of the crew, as well as the passengers, were drunk.

The next morning, the first mate managed to reach the shore in a small boat, and having secured it with a rope, it was possible to haul it back and forth, each time landing a few survivors: women and children first. Some were finally able to wade through the surf for over 100 yards, thus arriving on land soaking wet. That night, fires were lit, clothes were dried but few could rest. Provisions were few and it seemed that they were far from civilisation in a strange land inhabited by strange birds and kangaroos. They busied themselves chopping wood for fires, building some sort of shelter and hunting for food, while a few were dispatched to search for a lighthouse that the captain had reckoned was about thirty miles away.

After five days, there was concern that the men, who had been sent to search for the lighthouse, might be lost. In the meantime, the remainder had managed to repair the damaged lifeboat, so more men set out to reach the lighthouse by sea. Eventually, after six days, a man named Hickmot, arrived from the lighthouse; he had been alerted and he brought the good news that they hoped for. A steamer would arrive and take them to the mainland. On the seventh day, when provisions on the shore were running out, the single men, 116 in all, were informed that they were to set out and trek to the lighthouse, thirty miles away. One may assume that my great-grandfather was among their number. The trekking was not easy, through uncharted land, over sandhills, rocks, through the bush and up and down hills. Exhaustion began to win and some were tempted to return to the shore, when they saw the steamer heading that way. However, Hickmot reminded them that it was not big enough to hold them all and that a night in the comfortable beds in the lighthouse was a more attractive proposition. Rescue came a few days later in the form of the two other steamers, *Victoria* and *Phiros*. After a couple of days to recover at the lighthouse, they embarked on another fourteen mile trek back to the shore, where they were able to board the steamers. Some sailed directly to Melbourne, while others took the boat to Williamstown and then a train. Melbourne was ready for them where it is said that 'the people were very kind and gave them all they wanted'. One hundred and seventy remained there while the rest moved on to Brisbane. All seem to have survived their ordeal and signed a letter of gratitude to the Captain of the *Netherby*. John Valentine Watkins aged nineteen, is included on the passenger list! One would think that safe arrival would be enough, but no! My great-grandfather left his uncle and returned to England. We have no further knowledge of the uncle, but the resemblance of a man to my grandfather in my cousin's golf club in Sydney must be more than a coincidence, especially when his name turned out to be Watkins. Sadly, this man knew nothing of his background but claimed to be a New Zealander. Perhaps they moved on?

On John Watkins' return to England he became a master boiler-maker and worked as an iron ship's plater. He became an advocate of the nine-hour movement for factory workers, whilst sometime taking on the role of preacher of the Gospel.

Over the years there has been a long history of employers insisting on excessive hours for their work force. Factory reform came in steps. In 1802 it was decreed that children between the ages of nine to thirteen could work a maximum of eight hours a day, adolescents twelve hours a day and those under nine were not allowed to work. Factory owners were fined if they did not conform to the law. In actual fact, it was common for women and children to work as long as fourteen, sixteen or even eighteen hours a day in the cotton mills as late as 1816. Often this led to what we would call repetitive strain injuries such as housemaid's knee, bricklayer's elbow or tailor's ankle (Linsay 1996: *German Socialist Review*, 203, 'The time bandits, the fight for shorter hours'). Many more acts followed and by 1871–2 the Nine Hours Movement, which started in the North East of England, managed to cut further the ten-hour working day for adults who by then worked five and a half or six days a week (fifty-five to sixty hours a week), and achieved success after various strikes lasting four to five weeks which must have brought the hours down to nearer a fifty to fifty-four hour week.

John Watkins married and had four children, three girls and a son, my grandfather. His wife died in childbirth at the age of forty-two in 1890. One can only assume that he was devastated by the event. Certainly, from my grandfather's point of view it was the end of family life and his memories were of much greater fondness for his grandparents, the Kings. I never knew or heard talk of his father until he died in 1939. I suppose, without any factual backing, that he had taken to drink and squandered his money. Certainly, I do know that my grandfather would never have alcohol in the house.

George James Pedlar Watkins (my Grandpa Watkins, 1872–1964) my grandfather, was a lovely man; at least to me he was the epitome of everything that is good. He had had to fight for his position in life. As had most boys, in his young days he had had to leave school at the age of twelve, and thence earn his keep in any way that he could. He realised the importance of education and took himself off to night school to improve his learning. The sea must have been in his blood. His ambition in life was to join the Navy, but much to his disappointment he was turned down on the grounds of a lazy left eye. Fate had once again taken over in determining the continuation of our family. All those that were enlisted at that time, later went down in some disastrous submarine accident.

In 1896 Grandpa Watkins married my grandmother, Emily Alice Finch (1874–1949, Granny Watkins), in a church in Lewisham. I suspect that she was the brains of the family. A fine-looking woman, she was one of six children. Her brother Frank was noted for his mathematical abilities. It seems that he was awarded two civil decorations by the King for work in mathematics, and his patient vigilance of the clocks at the Greenwich Observatory, according to family comments, led to some minimal adjustment to the calendar that is still observed today. The need to introduce a leap year into the calendar had been recognised around 45 BC when Julius Caesar regulated the calendar. The astronomical calendar is not exactly 365.25 days but 365 days and 5 hours 48 minutes and 46 seconds (365.2422 days, meaning that there would be a full day's difference in 128 years). It is said by the family that he realised the calculations were out by a few seconds and that this has something to do with the fact that sometimes there is no leap year at the turn of the century. The truth of this matter is not fully understood.

My grandfather was said to be a boilermaker and shipbuilder, and worked for the major part of his adult life repairing the old Thames barges. The contract between himself and James Richard Piper of Pipers Wharf, East Greenwich was signed on 9 June 1903 when he was thirty-one. By the time he retired in 1932, he had been elected for life membership of Boilermakers and TSS Trades Union and was sufficiently comfortably off to donate his pension to another needy worker.

Granny and Grandpa produced two live children, preceded by twins, I believe, who died at birth. The girl was my Aunt Nell (Ellen Eliza Watkins, later Bean, 1899–1980s), the boy, my father, Frank James Watkins (1902–82). As a young boy, probably about six or seven, he developed a Perthés hip. The doctor advised that he should not weight-bear and for two years, my grandmother pushed him round in a wheelchair until the problem had healed. This paid dividends in that he could subsequently lead a normal life, including playing tennis and cricket, and it was not until much later in life that he suffered the pain of an arthritic hip.

Through his own misfortunes my grandfather realised the importance of education, not only for boys but also for girls. This emphasis has remained with the family right up until today.

Pride would have preferred him to maintain his daughter at home, but instead she trained as a schoolteacher and worked at the Macmillan School in Greenwich, amongst the poor, for a number of years before she married in her early thirties. It was a great sadness to her parents that marriage took her off to South Africa with her South African, Rhodes Scholar, husband, David Bean. After time in Johannesburg and Salisbury (Rhodesia), they finally followed their two sons who had moved and settled in Sydney, Australia. Ties were not completely broken as frequent trips to the UK kept them well in touch.

Equally my father was put through college for the study of civil engineering. His first posting was to the so-called 'white man's grave', to build the Apapa Wharf at Lagos, Nigeria. Not only did he survive the experience but so also did his houseboy. The lad had taken to his bed following a curse from the Witch Doctor, and was all set to die. My father managed to persuade him that the White Man's medicine was much better. A large dose of castor oil made it impossible for the boy to remain in bed any longer. The curse was overcome. My father always was a very practical man.

CHAPTER 3

My Jones ancestors
(1853 to twentieth century)

O UR KNOWLEDGE OF THE JONES family goes back to 1853, and the man who was my great-grandfather, a Stephen Jones, horse-brake builder and contractor in Greenwich, South East London. Although the first horse-drawn Hackney coaches and cabs are mentioned to be for hire on the streets of London in 1588, it was not until the mid-eighteenth century that their numbers began to swell and caused the now well known phenomenon of traffic congestion. By the time Steven Jones was in production, the main cabs were either the two-wheeled hansom that offered a 'fast and elegant' ride or the four-wheeled growler, said to be ponderous and which most commonly awaited the carriage of luggage from the railway stations. We know not what his particular craft produced, but he must have done enough to come to notice. It is said that he was the man who walked in front of the first car to drive through the Blackwall Tunnel at its opening in 1897. He carried the warning red flag. However, sadly for him, the coming of the motor car at the turn of the century was the end to what must have been a relatively prosperous career.

Stephen Jones married Ellen Worth in 1873 when she was twenty-three years old. As for many women in those days, life must have been one long string of pregnancies and loss. She died in 1891, having produced twelve children in short succession, the last in 1889. Of the twelve, five died in infancy, and another girl at the age of thirteen. Understanding old records is not easy. It seems that when a child died young, the next child was given the same name. This rather confuses the issue.

After the death of his first wife he remarried in 1893, a widow by the name of Elizabeth Matilda Homer, with a largish family of her own and who was said to be a 'rather formidable lady'.

My grandfather William George Jones (1874–1963) was the first born of the first marriage. He, with the remaining five, all lived to a ripe old age. William is listed as having been an engineer. We know not in what field but I understand that for some time he worked down at the Woolwich Arsenal where he was known as 'the peacemaker'. Known by us as a quiet, unassuming man, who was particularly good at finely slicing a loaf of bread when sandwiches were required for tea, it was he who apparently managed to calm upsets and fights in the workplace, without ever himself getting involved in the fighting. He was also renowned for his skill at removing foreign bodies from the eyes of his workmates. The special technique that he used was to pull a hair from the head of his patient and draw it across the surface of the eye and thus extracting the offending object.

William married my grandmother, Helen Batten (Grandma Jones), in 1897 at the Wesleyan Chapel in Leatherhead, her home town. She came from a strictly observing Wesleyan family. Her father was a Wesleyan preacher, as well as following his trade as a hairdresser. Her mother, Katharine (Worth), was daughter of a clockmaker. Katharine had previously been a court dressmaker before she settled for making home-made sweets. They managed to produce eleven children, two of whom died in infancy. From this background they brought up their family in rigid style. It was in the days when children should be seen and not heard and Sundays were strictly observed; no fun and games were allowed, apart from reading the Bible. I suppose I was considered lucky to be allowed to play tennis on a Sunday, providing I first went to church! In spite of all this, my aunt Dorothy, his granddaughter, remembers him as a 'jolly old man who used to sing a long song about a crocodile'; the last verse went like this:

And then one day, that crocodile
At last he took and died.
It took seven years to get him cold
He was so long and wide.
Chorus – Ri-fol, ri-fol etc

My grandmother's adaptations to married life from this sort of background must have been quite a shock. My grandfather came from a Methodist family but was somewhat less rigid in his views. Helen's prudish background and strong personality still dictated the rounded, curved legs of the dinner table must be covered in cloth, lest they might excite the men! Apart from this, the move to Greenwich and the London smoke, in place of the clean fresh air of the countryside around Leatherhead, caused her considerable health problems. She ailed a lot, and at one time was threatened with amputation of her leg, presumably for a non-healing ulcer. This offer was fiercely rejected and she remained intact for the rest of her life, apart from the distressing problems of deafness in later life. Communication was through an ear trumpet for most of the time, but in spite of this handicap, she continued to hold conversations at great distances, such as between upstairs and downstairs, and would be very cross with us if she could not hear our reply. My memories are of a lady of great character who loved jumble sales and always looked magnificent in one of her many hats.

Their first child, Dorothy, was born in 1901, followed by my mother Kitty (Margaret) in 1905. My mother was born prematurely, thanks to a traumatic accident. Burglars got into her parents' home, and managed to push my grandmother down the stairs, thus inducing a premature labour. Rumour has it that the doctor said 'you will never rear that child'. However, my grandmother, never one to obey instructions, not only managed to rear my mother but to rear someone who would survive for ninety-one years. The girls grew and moved on to school, my aunt to Haberdashers' Aske's at New Cross and my mother to the Roan School at Blackheath. Subsequently my aunt went to Homerton College, Cambridge, in order to train as a teacher of young children. My mother got a job at Liberty's, the famous London store in Regent's Street, where she worked for the years before marriage and became friendly with some of the girls who remained friends for the rest of her life.

In the pre-war years, came the time of William's retirement, but, it seems on an inadequate pension. Once again, my grandmother saved the day. They took on a shop in the town of Bookham, trading newspapers, sweets and toys. There is no doubt that she was the forceful element in this marriage. After a few years they managed to leave the shop and take on a house in Tonbridge, where they lived until they died in the 1960s. It was a small house, with a beautiful garden that they carefully and lovingly tended.

CHAPTER 4

The pre-war years (1932–39)

MEMORIES OF EARLY YEARS TEND to be fleeting and patchy. What is it that makes a particular situation or occasion stick in our minds? Three things seem to be common to mine – namely shock, disappointment and the warm feel of a happy family.

My first memory, probably at the age of about three and a half, is the moment when I looked out of the window of the French doors at our home in Canberra Road, Charlton. I can still see the image of the large rat as it ran across the garden from the fence to the garage. Maybe, in my memory, the rat is larger than life, but it was the sight of something that I instinctively knew was bad. A second memory is that of my fourth birthday, spent cooped up upstairs, in bed with what must have been the flu. A third is sitting on a stool in the kitchen, with a pudding basin on my head, while my mother cut my hair. Other vaguer pictures spring to mind of walks across the road to play in Charlton Park, but that is all.

More concrete memories have shaped since our move across the Heath when I was rising five years old. Our new house, No 51, was the first in Foxes Dale to be completed in the growing Cater Estate in Blackheath. The cost of the house in those days was a mere £1,000, at a time when one was comfortably off if one earned £1,000 a year. I understand that they now sell for nearly a million. It was ready for us just in time for me to take the big step of starting school. My mother was in hospital for that first day.

Health problems had afflicted her in those early days, although it was not until years later that I was to learn of her great distress. The promise of my parents of a new 'little brother or sister' had never materialised. I could never understand why their promise had not been fulfilled. In my ignorance I was unaware of the non-productive pregnancies: first a miscarriage and then a breech delivery, by her family doctor, at home of an 11 ½ lb stillborn boy. In this day and age, such a tragedy would not have occurred. A breech birth and such an enormous child would undoubtedly have been delivered in hospital with a very different outcome. However, they were not living in the litigious world of today. Far from suing their physician, my mother always considered him to be wonderful and followed his every instruction. Not long afterwards she developed Bell's Palsy, the disfigurement of which troubled her for the rest of her life; and then, on my first day at school she was in hospital for a hernia repair. I suppose many children are blind to their parents' traumas, while at the same time the parents are anxious to spare their children their pain.

It was Granny Watkins who took me on that first day. Dressed in my new school uniform, that allowed for plenty of room for growing, it was with some trepidation that I let go of her hand and went down the steps to reach the cloakroom. Suddenly, it was all too much and I reappeared outside the school, tearfully explaining that all the girls down there were so big . . . (some must have been at least six or seven!). In those days from 1936–9, the junior part of Blackheath High School was held at No 1, The Paragon, now a much sought after place for the wealthy to live. Our classes filled the building, and we had the benefit of a long garden that stretched down to a pond at the bottom. A great place to let off steam; although, never were we allowed to walk round the pond, unless accompanied by an adult. Many happy hours were spent in this garden, as well as the occasion on which we watched an outdoor performance of 'Hiawatha' put on by 'the big girls'. The headmistress of this Girls Public Day School Trust (GPDST) was Miss Lewis. She was of the old school. Formidable and seemingly unbending, she commanded respect and achieved results. Her heart was in the job and it showed.

For me, life in Foxes Dale was happy and untroubled. Every summer is remembered as being long, hot and sunny. Friends were entertained, both on the lawn and in the summerhouse, which was a particular haunt for dolls' tea parties and endless games of hospitals. It seems, that even at that stage, medicine was a particular fascination. By my fifth birthday, my father could wait no longer. Girl though I was, I had to have a Hornby train; hours were spent, as it raced around the track, cigarette in the funnel to simulate smoke, and screams of 'horrible accident' as it frequently left the rails and crashed on a bend.

More fun was had at the home of my grandparents (Granny and Grandpa Watkins). They had moved from 10 Hardy Road in

Blackheath to 14 Quernmore Road in Bromley. Our first car helped us to make the journey. They loved to entertain and with a large house and garden that included a tennis court, as well as an exciting wood at the bottom, everything was there to set the scene. Saturday afternoon tennis parties were the norm. The grown-ups talked, laughed, played tennis and took tea – plus my grandmother's special home-made ice cream. An added bonus for me, an only child, was my younger cousins who were all included in the numbers. The games of make-believe, bike rides, attempts at tennis and exploration of the wood formed bonds for me that have lasted all my life. My mother's sister, Dorothy, with young Susan and Roger, my father's sister, Aunt Nell, with my other cousins David and Andrew, who were temporarily in England on a long-stay visit from their home in Johannesburg, as well as a number of other 'extras' were able to make the most of this children's paradise.

I was once asked to recall the first meal that I could remember. I remember it clearly. I must have been about six when we were all gathered round the large table in my grandparents' home, for Christmas dinner. In the centre of the table was the decoration – a small house with Snow White and the Seven Dwarfs, popular at the time. Coloured lights lit the house. I still recall the moments of magic.

Sometimes we cannot be sure whether memories are our own or triggered by snapshots. I must have been about five when we had a family holiday down at Margate. We were all there: my four cousins together with all the parents and grandparents. While we played endlessly on the beach, paddled in the pools and tried to swim in the sea, our mothers sat on the sea wall, knitting. We still have the moving pictures, in colour, to prove it.

I was first introduced to the 'movies' when my grandparents returned from their trip round the world. Grandpa Watkins had worked all his life in the one company. His reliability and loyalty had raised him to the position where he could live in comfort. He retired at the age of sixty, and in 1934 fulfilled his lifelong dream of travelling the world. Staunchly British, and proud of it too, almost every visit was to be to those countries included in the British Commonwealth. He returned with endless film (black and white 8 mm), to regale us with their adventures, shared with their friends, the Macdonalds, as they circled the globe. The final high point, in fact he called it the 'masterpiece of the whole tour', was a flight from Paris in a small Hercules-type plane that looked almost as if it were tied together with string. The plane seated nineteen and took two and a quarter hours, flying at a speed of about 110 mph. It shows how things have moved on in the last seventy odd years. Then in 1934, he writes in his diary that prior to leaving Paris he 'rang up Frank and Kit in Charlton, London and we hear their voices clearly; fancy speaking from a Paris bedroom to your friends in a home in London! What would the Pharaohs have thought of that?'

Maybe it was all this that stimulated my interest in travel – or perhaps in a family like ours, it was in the blood. However, I do remember clearly my grandfather's film of Rotorua in New Zealand. A man was seen catching a fish in one pool and whisking it across to another hot pool to cook it. Of course, I had to go there.

Home entertainment was the thing in those days. Radio and the old, wind-up HMV gramophone there was, but with no television, DVD or iPod. It was a case of 'do it yourself'. In addition to the films of Grandpa's travels, he would hire reels from the local store. The favourite was Charlie Chaplin – silent, of course. Repeatedly we called for a rerun of the film in which Charlie's ice cream slipped from his plate on an upper balcony and fell down the front of a woman's evening dress on the balcony below. More laughter followed as he then ran the film backwards. The ice cream neatly returned to Charlie's plate.

These were good times. We were fiercely loyal to our country. In 1937, we celebrated the coronation of King George VI in style, dressed in red, white and blue and waving the Union Jack to show allegiance to our new King. By this time too, I had a new friend, a beautiful red cocker spaniel by the name of Laddie. He was mine and I loved him.

Life was safe, happy and secure. Modern changes had not arrived. The lamplighter appeared each evening at dusk to light the lamp outside our door; friends still had gas lighting in their home. At Sainsbury's, the grocers in Blackheath village, butter did not come in half pound packets (or even one of 250 g); the man behind the counter picked up the wooden butter pats, carved off a chunk and shaped it before wrapping it up himself. Hinds, the drapery store, thought themselves to be very modern, with electrically operated caskets that could be passed on wires overhead to the cash desk, money inside, and returned with the change, and Woolworth's really was the store in which nothing was sold over the price of sixpence, and they dealt in a wide variety of goods for this minimal cost.

I was blissfully unaware of the build-up to what lay ahead. The only recognition of the fact that things might go wrong was the night of 30 November 1936. I had previously been driven past the impressive, vast Crystal Palace at Sydenham. The large, imposing glass structure stretched 1,848 ft by 408 ft. They promised that one day we would go to visit it. That night in 1936 put an end to all such thoughts. I was called to the window of my parents' bedroom to see the whole sky glowing red from the flames that demolished the building once and forever. Perhaps life was not so safe and secure as I had imagined.

CHAPTER 5

The war years (1939–45)

AT SEVEN YEARS OF AGE, the world is one's home – or at least it was for me. Mutterings of impending war had no meaning nor did I have any understanding of how such an event would affect my happy and secure way of life. The first awareness that 'something was happening' was the day when my Laddie rushed down the garden, barking furiously. Looking upwards I could see his cause for alarm. There, against the background of a clear blue sky, was a strange object. I was told it was a barrage balloon, 'rehearsing' for its job of interception of expected low flying enemy aircraft. The dog did not like it, a fact that caused a certain unease in me. Next was the trying on of gas masks, a rather claustrophobic experience, worsened by the overpowering smell of rubber. All the family was involved and, worried though they must have been, my parents managed to make light of it as we later packed them away in their small cardboard boxes. Finally, having never before been to the cinema, we went down the road to Lee Green, two days running, to see *Snow White*, the story of which I was already a fan. It was the next day when all ears seemed to be pinned to the radio. A chill still runs through me as I listen to the recording of the speech of Neville Chamberlain on 3 September 1939. The serious tone of the voice was clear as he uttered the words:

> I am speaking to you from the Cabinet Room at 10, Downing Street. This morning the British Ambassador in Berlin handed the German Government a final note stating that unless we heard from them by 11.00 a.m. that they were prepared at once to withdraw their troops from Poland, a state of war would exist between us.
>
> I have to tell you that no such undertaking has been received, and that consequently this country is at war with Germany.

That day, it was goodbye to the house and all that was in it, my school, my friends, my Laddie and the budgerigars, Tweedledum and Tweedledee. Life was never to be the same again. Afraid that London would immediately be a target for bombing, my mother and I left for Leighton Buzzard in Bedfordshire. We were to stay in the home of my mother's Aunt Jenny and Uncle Jack, together with Mum's sister, Dorothy and my cousins Roger and Susan. I was pleased to be with my cousins once again but no doubt we created untold problems for our hosts; this Victorian couple were well set in their ways. It cannot have been easy for them to adapt to a sudden influx of disturbed children and worried adults. For six weeks we went to a small school nearby, played round the house and shocked Uncle Jack, when four-year-old Susan came downstairs in her pyjamas. He appeared to be no happier when we decided to play 'Babes in the Wood' in his neat and tidy workshop. The influx of the leaves required to cover ourselves did not seem to meet with his approval.

Within weeks we were once again on the move. This time it was to Dorking where my father apparently had a job. For another six weeks the three of us settled into a house whose walls were decorated with scrawls of ink, and I went to another school nearby. Certain changes can have a lifelong effect. For me at the age of eight, I had just mastered the great achievement of joined-up writing, and was so proud of it. At this new school, I was not allowed to do it. Maybe, this is a good excuse for the fact that most people today find my handwriting completely illegible. I say most people, but I have to admit that I too have great difficulty in deciphering it.

Many people today would consider that we were lucky during the war. None of our family were in the Services because they were protected by reserved occupations, my father as a civil engineer, and my uncle as a doctor in Rochester. Unlike so many, our families remained untouched by loss. Neither were we reft from our families to be put on trains, carrying a small bags of toothbrush, clothes and gas mask, to strange places and strange people during the evacuation of the children from the expected dangers in London. The transfer of my father to a job in Cumberland must have been seen as a gift from heaven. He was posted to build a TNT factory in the small village of Drigg. We moved, *en bloc*, to the next door village of Seascale along the coast. We, together with Dorothy, Roger and Sue were joined by both sets of grandparents. Both grandfathers joined the ranks of 'Dad's Army' enlisting in the Home Guard. Each evening they donned their tin hats and bore their gas masks to the water tower in the village to be 'on watch'. We never heard much about what went on there but I suspect a fun time was had by all. Raids and bombing were few and far between in this far off spot. However, we did have our blitz. Barrow-in-Furness, south of us, was subjected to a number of heavy attacks. Planes that had not dropped all their bombs occasionally shed the extras on us. Three times I recall the loud explosions that followed but fortunately they, as well as the odd damaged plane that crashed, missed the village and fell on open land. It's strange how some happenings leave lasting impressions. I could still point to the page, exactly half way down the page, in the book, *What Katy Did*, that I was reading at the moment the first bomb fell with a resounding bang.

Adversity, somehow, seems to draw people together. The 'wartime spirit' was in full force here. Our family, together with those families of my father's colleagues, grateful for the supposed safety of this haven, settled to an active social life that allowed lifelong friendships to develop, with parties at our new home, Walden Heath, and beach hut on the dunes. The war was not forgotten, as we knitted scarves 'for the soldiers' and later were involved in delivering the mail, a service that was hampered by the loss of manpower, as local postmen had been called up.

Our actual arrival in Seascale was not so promising. Tired after the long twelve to fourteen hour train journey from London, we eventually dismounted and crossed the bridge against an icy cold wind and the early signs of a snowstorm. The locals tried to reassure us with the words, 'The snow never lays here'. How wrong they were. For six long weeks we were trapped by the heavy fall. Everything was white, with roads and the railway, unrecognisable under drifts that filled the track between the high hedges on either side.

The welcome to our new abode was not promising. The pipes were frozen and we had no running water. Central heating did not exist and the only source of heat was the kitchen range that must be cleared and lit each morning or an open fire in the grate. It must have been a nightmare for my mother in a house full of people. Snow had to be melted down to get some supply of water, and we were sent each morning about half a mile across the golf course to fetch drinking water from the small spring that kept going there. Carrying jugs and buckets, we made our daily trek. Unlike today, life did not come to a standstill. My father continued to go to work, we walked to school and did our lessons in greatcoats and gloves and when there was no ambulance to lift the man with appendicitis to hospital, he was carried manually across the drifts until they reached a road some miles away that had been cleared.

For the first few months of the war, we had the benefit of the car. It did not last. The petrol allowance for private motoring was stopped and we were reliant on bicycles, Shanks's pony and the train. We had done one journey from London to Seascale, in the car, in order to transport some essentials and to have the car for use there. I remember a rather tense journey with frequent references to the map. All the road signs had been taken down in case of invasion by the enemy. They wanted to ensure that any invaders became instantly lost. No doubt it was a good idea but was no help to us, making this long 300-mile journey for the first time through strange country. However, we did eventually make it and were then able to take advantage of the vehicle in those first few months of the war before petrol rationing was introduced. With it we explored some of the surrounding areas with visits to Eskdale, Buttermere and Crummock Water and Ennerdale. It was at the hotel at the head of the latter that we heard on the radio, the first speech in 1940 made by the then Princess Elizabeth, our present Queen. We walked for miles round lakes, over hills and up mountains. Once petrol was no longer available, our trips were confined to bicycle rides to the head of Wastwater and thence up Stye Head Pass to the tarn at the top. Wastwater is my favourite lake. The deepest of all the lakes, it is surrounded by the peaks of Great Gable, Kirk Fell and Scafell Pike and edged on one side by the grey, forbidding screes. Magnificent at all times it has a particular grandeur in the light of black clouds on a stormy day.

Near home we could walk along the beach as far as Sellafield, unspoiled at that time by the towers of the nuclear power station that stand there today. The only other escape was a fourteen-mile journey on the train to the nearest town of Whitehaven. Shops, cinema, fish and chips and ice cream at Mrs Batty's were our special treats there, away from the isolation of Seascale. Our view of the Lake District was further extended towards the end of the war when we managed two short holidays at Derwentwater, another beautiful spot. Staying in the now luxurious Lodore Hotel, we walked and walked, often round the lake, crossing the Cat Bells range of mountains on the other side. It always felt like a great achievement.

Time moved on. The job at Drigg was complete and my father relocated to work on the Mulberry Harbour, some of which was being built on the Erith Marshes, near Woolwich in London. He was back amongst the dangers, bombing, Doodlebugs (V1) and rockets (V2). Working by day, nights were spent on the roof of his office at 3 St James's Place, in London, fire-watching. Some of this time my mother felt she must be at his side, so I was left to board at the school. I was once again, the only child and now separated from the family, apart from Granny and Grandpa Watkins, who had bought a house up there. They became my greatest support.

On arrival in Seascale I had started at the Calder Girls School – otherwise known as 'Miss Wilson's School for Young Ladies'. I was told that I was lucky that there was such a good school nearby. Educationally, I suppose, this was true but somehow I did not fit in. To start with I was a day girl at a boarding school and secondly I came from the south and was different from all the other girls who were either Scottish or came from the north. However, there was one bonus of joining the northerners. They celebrated Halloween. Unnoticed in those days down south, here it was a most important occasion and celebrated in style. The night before a notice would go up in the Common Room to say that, on the night of 31 October, all our teachers would be going out and that we would be left in charge of the witch, the cat and the bat. We were instructed to assemble in the Common Room at 6 p.m. When we arrived at the appointed hour, the room was in semi-darkness, lit by only a few candles. The cloaked witch, winged bat and tailed cat flitted round. Their costumes were supposed to disguise our teachers who were reputed to have left the building. We sat in a semi-circle for tea. Each course was introduced by a short poem before we feasted on things like bats eggs (baked potatoes in their jackets), and little girls' bones (cheese straws). They put on a truly magical event.

The other memorable entertainment at the school were the musicals put on by two of the teachers, Miss Gardner and Miss Bellamy in the senior school. Somehow, in these restricted times they managed first class productions of *The Mikado* and *Ruddigore*. All must take part. At this time of my life I was desperately shy and obviously not suitable for an important part. Nevertheless, a place was found for me, behind a sheet appropriately lit, as a shape!

By the time I moved across the road to the senior school, the war was at its height and times were hard. Strict food rationing was in force and the school allowed us no extras, apart from a birthday cake once a year. We did not go without, in fact, the wartime diet was a very healthy one. However, apart from one sweet (or four Smarties) after lunch, goodies were not on the menu. We had to eat what was on offer or go hungry. I recall endless meals of what we called 'slosh and horsemeat' – basically a stew of gristle and gravy, followed by 'murder on the Alps' (semolina pudding with red jam on top). For breakfast we were allowed one teaspoonful of sugar. The dilemma was how to use this precious allowance. My solution was to give up sugar in my tea, have salt on my porridge and save the sugar to have on my bread. The luxury of jam was reserved for Sundays. Even though bread was not actually rationed during the war, there were times when it was in short supply. Queues formed outside the shops in the early morning and there was no guarantee that there would be enough for all. This must have affected the school during the time when, at teatime we were reduced to two half slices of bread and a scrape of margarine and if we were really hungry we could have one more half slice with no spread. Not to be beaten, I resorted to mustard. I have never liked it since. The luxury of bananas and oranges was non-existent. In the whole of the war, I was treated to one orange. I have to say it was the most delicious orange I have ever tasted. On the down side was tinned figs for tea. I have never eaten another fig since.

Rationing in the Second World War was first introduced on 8 January 1940. Initially it was restricted to bacon, butter and sugar but meat, tea, jam, biscuits, breakfast cereals, cheese, eggs, milk and canned fruit were soon added. Amounts varied at different times but the following is a table taken from Wikipedia 2010, 'Rationing in the United Kingdom'. At a time of food shortages we were all encouraged to 'dig for victory' and to grow our own vegetables. With the meagre meat ration, new recipes appeared based on the products from our gardens and allotments, and when butter and margarine could not be spared for baking, a plethora of recipes for fatless cakes became available. Old habits die hard. Even now, nearly seventy years later, I find myself rinsing out the milk bottle to extract the last few drops of the precious liquid.

Item	Maximum level Per week unless otherwise stated	Minimum level Per week unless otherwise stated	Rations April 1945 Per week unless otherwise stated
Bacon and ham	8oz (227g)	4oz (113g)	4oz (113g)
Sugar	16oz (454g)	8oz (227g)	8oz (227g)
Loose tea	4oz (113g)	2oz (57g)	2oz (57g)
Meat	1s 2d approx 1lb 3oz (540g)	1s	1s 2d
Cheese	8oz (227g)	1oz (28g)	2oz (57g)
Preserves	1lb (0.45kg) per month	8oz (227g) per month	2lb (0.91kg) marmalade or 1lb preserve or 1lb sugar
Butter	8oz (227g)	2oz (57g)	2oz (57g)
Margarine	12 oz (340g)	4oz (113g)	4oz (113g)
Lard	3oz (85g)	2oz (57g)	2oz (57g)
Sweets	1lb (454g) per month	8oz (227g per month)	12oz(340g) per month
Eggs	1 egg or a packet of dried egg per week. 1 packet equivalent to 12 eggs.		

The school was always terrified of infection that might spread amongst the pupils. Our first day back from holidays was devoted to 'nit' inspection. Train carriages and buses were deemed to be 'alive' with the creatures and the fear was that we might introduce lice to the school and the school might develop a bad reputation. We all sat, for what seemed like hours, while the hair was carefully searched with a fine toothed comb.

One term, I disgraced myself by returning to school with a cough, a nasty cough that went on and on. Looking back, I have no doubt that it was the dreaded whooping cough, but the school would never admit to it. However, to be on the safe side I was admitted to the san. (sanatorium or sick bay). For a whole term I was imprisoned there. On the odd occasion they let me out, one cough and I was back, stuck there alone once more. It was a bad time for me. In this solitary confinement, I was lonely and miserable. Friends and my grandparents were not allowed to visit me and I had mental pictures of my parents and my Laddie in London, constantly at risk from the bombing. Not surprisingly, when I eventually returned to the classroom, I could not keep up with the work and my school report was such that my father took me to one side and said, 'This will not do'. For me this was no help. I could not catch up and with the constant disapproval I was unhappy.

There were a few times during the war when I was allowed back to London and home; times when the raids had quietened and it was deemed to be a bit safer. Home was the place that I always wanted to be. I could catch up with a few friends and see my dog, although he had been taken over by the next-door neighbours, who by then considered him to be theirs, but Laddie himself never forgot me. Quiet though the war was at that time there were still reminders. At night, I lay in bed listening to the drone of British planes flying off on their bombing missions and the stomach-turning, piercing wail of the air-raid siren, warning of approaching enemy aircraft. One such alarm occurred in the middle of a small gathering that had been arranged to celebrate my birthday. Our house was blessed with a Morrison shelter. The steel-topped table with cage surround was there to protect us should the house be hit. The size of a large double bed, it was somewhat overcrowded as we crammed in to the small space and there continued the party. Later in the days of the doodlebugs (the pilotless planes released over London by the Germans), it spared my father when he was sleeping in it on the night the missile demolished a house a couple of doors away. The reassuring buzz of the plane caused fear for those below, more terrifying was when the engine cut out and no one could know where it would land. Our house, like every other house in the borough of Greenwich, was badly damaged. It was a particularly vulnerable area as many V1 and V2 dropped short of Central London and the anti-aircraft battery placed on the heath brought down many of the planes heading into town. The rubble from those times now fills the large dips that once could be seen on Blackheath. The annual Blackheath Fair is now held on one of these filled in dips. Before the war it was held in a dip that was so deep that the only visible part of the fair was the top of the helter-skelter.

Eventually, the great day came. London had quietened and it looked as if the war was coming to an end. D-Day, on 6 June 1944, had led the way. At last I took my final journey from Seascale. As I looked out of the carriage window at the familiar grey, windswept sea, I remember my over-riding thought, 'I hope I never see the sea again'.

My return to normality was not immediate. I was to rejoin my old school, Blackheath High, which during the war had been evacuated to Tunbridge Wells. For that summer term, I lodged with my maternal grandparents (Grandma and Grandad), who were living in Tonbridge, and took the bus each day to the school. From that moment, everything looked up. I dropped a class, which allowed me to catch up with the work. Instead of constantly coming bottom of the class, I began to be at the top. Sport too began to be an important part of my life.

VE day came on 8 May 1945 and was greeted by great celebrations. The capitulation of the Japanese and war in the Far East quickly followed on 15 August 1945, after the unleashing of the atomic bombs on Hiroshima (6 August 1945) and Nagasaki (9 August 1945). We were down in the New Forest to celebrate the end of the war that was supposed to end all wars. If only it had. We joined the crowd round the bonfire on Brockenhurst Common and released a rocket that had been saved through the whole war by an elderly lady in our hotel, just for such an occasion.

CHAPTER 6

Home at last (1945–9)

I WAS FOURTEEN, A TEENAGER but a very different teenager from the ones we see on our streets today. Far from wanting to go against authority and flee the nest, I was content to be at home and settle down to the family routine. However, home was not quite the same place that I had left five years before. The war had left its mark. War damage had to be repaired, new friends established and Laddie was no longer my dog. The Bristows, next door, had taken him on for all those war years and, although I was always welcomed in, it was not quite the same. Thinking back one cannot understand why it mattered so much but, just before the war I had been given a round jigsaw. For some reason it was special. I had never before had a round jigsaw, all my others had been the conventional rectangles. The war came before I had had the opportunity to complete it. I suppose, for all those years away, I had dreamed of returning and completing the puzzle. What a disappointment to find, on my return, that my mother had had a good turn out and thrown it away. Some things are hard to forgive!

Rationing was not to end for some years, in fact in some commodities it was even more stringent. We had been through the bread shortages of the war but supplies were actually rationed from 1946 to 1948, and were continued for sugar und sweets until 1953 and meat and bacon until 1954. We had become used to clothing coupons that basically restricted our choices to essentials such as school uniforms and shoes. Amounts varied with sixty-six points in 1942, forty-eight in 1943 and only twenty-four in 1945. Bearing in mind that a man's suit required twenty-six to twenty-nine coupons, a fully lined overcoat eighteen or a pair of women's shoes seven, it did not in any way encourage us to be following the latest fashions. Motoring, which had been taboo for the private individual since the early period of the war, did not immediately return. Initially there were limited supplies and rationing was not finally lifted until May 1950. Public transport included the old trams from Lee Green to

Lewisham, buses, and trains, but with less traffic on the road, bikes were in common use. This was fine, until the wheels of the bike got caught on the rut of a tramline.

Blackheath High School had moved back to its old site in time for the autumn term. By this time I had moved up into the senior school, so my last years there were in Wemyss Road. Each day I cycled to school, caught up with a few old friends and made new ones. School routine took shape, but we were not pampered. No one had heard of central heating. Some winters in those days were severe, and I have vivid memories of attending classes in winter coat, cap and gloves to study in a room that was heated only by a very small open fire in the corner of the room. However, it was not all bad. Christmas traditions still held with the magic of the carol service each year in the hall. As we sat in the darkened hall, the choir would enter by the cross shaped stone steps at the end, carrying candles and singing 'The First Noel'.

It was at this point that sport became a major interest for me. In the north, we had played both hockey and lacrosse. My preference was for hockey, but thanks to a disagreement with a prefect taking a game on the beach, I was banned from the game and forced to play lacrosse instead. Our only sin had been to request a rest at half-time on a rather inclement day of wind and drizzle. When the girl refused our request, we all sat down. She reported us to the head, and the punishment was meted out. Those of us who preferred lacrosse must play hockey in future, but those, like myself who most enjoyed hockey, must take the other option. Little did they foresee the benefit of this for me on my return to London where lacrosse was being introduced to the school for the first time. No one else had ever played the game before. As an old hand, I was immediately promoted to the first team and continued there until the end of my schooldays, finishing as vice-captain. Not satisfied with that I played in all the other teams in netball, rounders and tennis and loved it.

My tennis career was encouraged by the Priory Lawn Tennis and Squash Club that lay across the road from us in Foxes Dale. It became a regular haunt of mine, as well as many of 'us youngsters'. We were noticed and entered for the Junior Kent Championships held at Beckenham, as well as the opportunity of some free lessons from a Captain Rogers. Although tennis was great, it required time and good weather. Thus the squash courts at the club became an even greater haven. Ruth Turner, who played squash for England, took on the task of initiating us into the sport. We met regularly; I took immediately to the game which eventually led to success in the British Junior Championships (under twenty-one), in 1951. In the final I managed to beat Shirley Bloomer who was at the point of deciding whether to make her career in tennis or squash. Her later successes in tennis must mean that she made the right choice. My reward for winning was six lessons with the then World Champion, Mamhoud Karim. There followed a win at the West of England Championships held at Exmouth, being entered for the Women's British Championships held at the Lansdowne Club in London, captaincy of the London University team, and gaining first a half purple and later a full purple there, as well as playing second string in the Kent team. Much fun was enjoyed over the years in a sport that could be played in a short time, at any time of the day or late into the evening and in any weather. An end to all this came when back problems and a young family made it too difficult to continue, but later I had the joy of teaching them to play and, of course, once again catching the bug, playing on the club ladder and in the club team.

Encouraged by the better understanding of lessons, progress continued at school and as I achieved sufficient results in the School Certificate examination, thoughts began to stray on to my next move. With a liking for biology and the sciences, my inclinations were towards nursing. However, with my father's awareness of the advantages of a college education, he suggested, 'Why don't you go to college and learn how to be a doctor?' In those days one listened to, and followed this parental advice which led me to embark on a lifetime of interest in a job that I loved. In those days one could enter Medical School with the School Certificate examination only. Should one have actually achieved Higher Certificate in the right subjects and at the right grades one could actually move straight on to the Second MB course. I was accepted with School Certificate only and took the equivalent as First MB at the college. As I left the school in the summer of 1949, I stood at the doorway and hesitated before taking the next step into the rest of my life.

CHAPTER 7

My early years in medicine (1949–55)

M Y FIRST INTRODUCTION TO THE Royal Free Hospital Medical School at 8 Hunter Street, London, was at my initial interview. Women in medicine in those days were still very much in the minority. The concept of women in medicine had been slow to be accepted. Although over the centuries they had been regarded as comforting healers, their skills were mainly turned to that of the midwife, unless by some stroke of luck, and a family male tutor, they found ways of practising in secret. In the UK, it was not until 1870, after years of struggle and rejection, that Elizabeth Garrett (Anderson, after marriage), finally received the MD degree, the licence to practise, and subsequently served as Dean for twenty years, at the London School of Medicine for Women. More women have qualified and been accepted and have worked since that time. The war years heralded the opportunity for women to practise their skills as in so many other trades in which men had previously had the monopoly; with the men away in the Services, women had, of necessity, to fill the gaps. By 1949, at the time that I started, the great step of admitting women to most of the medical schools was just getting going. The previously male bastions were opening their doors to a quota of ten per cent of women. Equally, the Royal Free had reciprocated with the offer of places for ten per cent of men. One or two lone males had been accepted in the previous couple of years and we had the increased numbers of four in our year.

Having been already rejected by Guys, I was not particularly confident as I arrived at the doors of the Medical School. However, they must have been satisfied with my CV, references and responses to their questions, strange though they might have seemed. Three questions stick out in my mind: the first, what books did I read? A bit of a problem as I have always tended to be a doer rather that a great reader. My main memories of reading when young were the Just William stories and Arthur Ransom and the adventures of a group of children in the Lake District. Secondly, what did I think about the new Health Service that had been launched on 5 July 1948? Difficult, as I knew that everyone was not happy with the changes. The other question was, who did I go to the cinema with? Anyway, whatever I managed to think up, it was accepted and I was granted a place at the school into the first year, to take the First MB examination in biology, physics and chemistry.

The first few years in the study of medicine were the hardest, at least for me. Anatomy, physiology, organic chemistry and pharmacology for Second MB were a pretty hard slog that required stamina and a good memory. The timetable was filled with lectures, practical work in the laboratory and the study of human anatomy as we, bit by bit, dissected the human body. I wonder how today they manage it, now that there is so much in-depth understanding of how everything actually works! All went well until the dreaded exam. Much to my embarrassment, my knowledge and memory for pharmacology completely dried up. I obviously had not properly prepared and failed miserably. A downside of this was that all my friends moved on and I was left for six months to repeat the study of this one subject that I did not enjoy. On the other hand it was a salutary lesson, and never again did I present myself at an examination unprepared.

Life looked up when I moved to the hospital in Grays Inn Road where I was involved with clinical work and the constant fascination of patients and their problems. Here we gained experience on the wards, spent time at Lawn Road during our fevers stint and lived in over our maternity placement. Medicine has changed a lot since those days. Then, we saw diseases that rarely seem to occur today. The saddest were the young, dying from the heart damage they suffered following attacks of rheumatic fever, or those stricken by the effects of polio before the days of the polio vaccine. Without the benefit of stents, heart bypass operations or even transplants, not to mention the plethora of medications to suit every purpose, bad cases of angina and heart attacks sounded the death knell. Although Fleming had discovered penicillin as early as 1928, it was not until the war that it was really put into clinical use together with the old M&B used in the treatment of gonorrhoea. In the 1950s we were emerging; now we seemed to practise in another world. However, in spite of the fact of modern medicine, some things are not as they were. In those days people were grateful, respect for the profession was pretty universal and the question of litigation a rarity. Most doctors played their part by dedicating themselves to the profession, working long hours and working, not just for the money, but for the benefit of the patient.

Finally, I qualified with MRCS LRCP and MB BS degrees in 1955. While awaiting my first posting I filled in as a locum at the maternity unit of the Elizabeth Garrett Anderson Hospital at Hampstead. The vacancy occurred at the time of the disruption caused by the epidemic of the so-called 'Royal Free disease'. Most of my year and many of the medical staff and nurses were affected. Not only did they have to endure the worrying symptoms of this disease but also the implied shame, as some labelled the problem to be one of mass hysteria. By now, their plight has been vindicated as the current thought is that this was an epidemic of myalgic encephalitis (ME). I was lucky in that we were on holiday at that particular time and so did not go down with it.

My first real job after qualification was in obstetrics at the Liverpool Road branch of the Royal Free Hospital. Here we were thrown in at the deep end. Working a 108-hour week and sleeping on the job, we were expected to cope for the remuneration of £5 per week, less £1.50 for our board and lodging. Complaints gained no sympathy from our bosses who claimed that, in their day they had had no time off and were not paid for their services. We were told that we were lucky to have our half day each week, starting at noon – if we had finished – and ending at midnight, and alternate weekends, starting at noon on the Saturday – if we had finished – and ending at midnight in the Sunday. My opposite number and I decided to cover each other so that we could stay off until the Monday morning. Sadly I was caught out and threatened that I would lose my job if it ever happened again. Hard though it was for us, there is no disputing the fact that we were on a quick learning curve in taking responsibility, and crammed a wealth of experience into a short time. One wonders in this age of various EU directives, restricted hours or paid overtime for extras, how medical students and doctors will manage to emerge with the same breadth of view.

CHAPTER 8

The marriage (1955–84)

URING MY LAST FEW YEARS at college, my thoughts turned to home life and marriage. Michael and I met at the squash club and enjoyed each other's company. Here was someone who was actually asking me what I would like to do. The relationship developed and in 1951, at the top of the big wheel at the Blackheath Fair, he asked me to marry him. The answer, of course, was yes and the wedding day eventually fixed for 7 July 1956, after we had both completed our training; he a chartered accountant and myself, a fully fledged doctor. The marriage took place at the Congregational Church on Burnt Ash Hill, Lee, reception at the Bromley Court Hotel and honeymoon at Langton Matravers in Dorset, where my new husband had lived as a child. We enjoyed a great day, helped along by the company and good wishes of the family and many good friends.

Looking back, one realises that one's expectations of marriage are very much based on one's previous experiences, but in the naiveté of youth, one assumes that one's future partner has the same ideas on life. My expectations were based on the security of a loving and united family. When my grandfather used to say about himself and Granny Watkins, 'Not many people have got what we have,' I really did not know what he meant. For me, their happiness was normal. On the other hand, when my mother did happen to mention the shocking event of divorce, the implication was that someone had done something dreadful and failed in their input into the partnership. Marriage must be for life and any hiccups along the way should be sorted by mutual discussion.

Michael and I were probably doomed to failure from the beginning. He had grown up with an absent father who was serving throughout the war as an orthopaedic surgeon, abroad in the army. As he said, his father was a man he never knew. His mother (Pip) and the two boys, John and Michael had returned to England at the start of the war. They had left behind their early years in the Far East, where they were often cared for by *amahs* (nursemaids), while Pip joined in the army social life and bridge parties. On their return to England, Pip shouldered all responsibility of coping in their new home in Dorset in strange surroundings. Years later, when I knew her in Blackheath, I found it hard to understand her need to make a point of taking her 'half day'. It was almost as if she was an employee in the home. She used her time to go to visit her brother on the other side of London. The boys never really had the opportunity to experience a full family life. Both were sent off to boarding schools at an early age, and Michael never had the advantage of knowing the role of men and fathers in the home, other than the fact that they supported the family financially.

The blessing of our liaison was the children; Janet born in 1958, Carol 1962 and Andrew 1966. My father had been an important feature of my childhood, so naturally, I wanted Michael to be the same for them. Sadly, my repeated efforts to achieve this failed and my increasing efforts to hold together the 'happy home' were never enough. My consequent depression hung heavy but, fortunately, to some extent, was somewhat counteracted by the joy of my growing family and my job. At least there, I had someone saying thank you and well done.

Married life was started in a flat in Lee at 7 Birch Grove. I feel we were lucky in that the wide variety of gadgets that is felt to be necessary today was not available in 1956. We were able to appreciate the benefits of modern developments as they came along, one by one. The only luxury in this first flat was a small fridge. There was hot water, but in the bathroom only, and initially no Hoover. It was a case of down on one's hands and knees with a dustpan and brush, until the labour-saving, more efficient carpet-sweeper came along. However, when the magic Hoover did arrive, it had been made to last. Things were repaired in those days and not discarded. It was not cheaper to buy a new one. My old treasure, the Hoover Junior, lasted me twenty-six years. However, I can't believe how stupid I must have been to object to the acquisition of a washing machine when Jan was on the way. I did give in to pressure but insisted on washing all the nappies by hand, in case the machine spoiled them. Gradually, after our move to Martins, at Willow Grove, Chislehurst we were able to add the extra labour-saving devices as they came along.

When it came to television, one has to bear in mind that it was the Coronation in 1952 that first proved the main stimulus for people to have a television in the home. I had seen one as early as 1937, in a shop window in Blackheath Village, but the thought of ever possessing one was a pipe dream. My parents eventually acquired their first, black and white model to watch the procession and service that anointed Princess Elizabeth as our Queen Elizabeth II. It was not until 1958, that we finally had a set in our home at Chislehurst. Colour did not arrive until after Andrew's birth some fourteen years later.

When Janet arrived, I had planned to cut work back to fit in with family life and perhaps take on a few part-time baby clinics. However, I realised early that somehow I would have to be self-reliant. General practice seemed to be the avenue that would allow me to support the family and be Mum at the same time. For me it turned out to be a lifesaver. I loved the job, enjoyed the company of my work colleagues and still could work my hours, as far as possible, around the children, with the help of a string of au pairs and home helps.

Fortunately, in those days we were not really aware of the possibility of problems of child abuse. Police checks on those involved with children were not required, and we had no guilt or anxieties about leaving the children in their care, especially as it allowed for me to be free for them when I was at home. In general we were lucky, but nevertheless things did not always run smoothly. Starting with a delightful Danish girl, Lena, recommended by a family friend, who settled in and coped well, not only with Jan as a baby but also the new dog Bobby. We had decided to treat him as a dog and not to pamper him. He had settled nicely in a kennel in the garden. Lena felt sorry for him, brought him into her room, on to the bed, and wrapped him in her best winter coat. He never went near the kennel again. After a few months, the worries began. Lena was pregnant. We decided that providing her parents were involved, she could stay with us. The parents came over and she continued the pregnancy in our home, with the desperately sad outcome of having to leave the child at the hospital for adoption afterwards. I shall never forget the look on her face as she said goodbye. Lena was followed by Ritva from Finland, an English girl Julia, and Maryse from France before a succession of others. We and the children became very fond of these girls and partings were sometimes hard but one realised that, at the end of the day it was family continuity that mattered most. I was also lucky in that on numerous occasions and in situations of crisis, my parents were always able to come to the rescue.

As the children got older we could rely on daily helps to take over the caring. We moved from our house at 57 Abergeldie Road, Lee to 67 Hervey Road and the girls went to my old school of Blackheath High and Andrew, first to Riverstone and thence to St Dunstan's School at Catford. Mrs Wallace, who cared for the family after school, became a family friend, and Jenny Farmer a friend and adopted aunt. Together we had much fun, especially as we gathered in the kitchen to prepare for yet another celebration. Christmas, birthdays, Jan and Carol's weddings, my parents Golden Wedding and eventually our twenty-fifth wedding anniversary all had to be catered for, but in our lovely home at 67 Hervey Road, our joint efforts were all part of the festivities. No, married life was not all bad. Home entertaining was the thing, doing the rounds of our friends for dinner parties and sometimes a game of bridge, not to mention the following of the opera that Michael loved. It was great to see it played at Sadler's Wells or Covent Garden performed by top class singers.

These years were not without their traumas. We managed to have two fires during our years at Hervey Road. The first was not long after the birth of Andrew. An ex-neighbour's daughter, Christine had upset her family by becoming pregnant. She came to live with us, and so enabled me to return to work a little earlier than I might have done otherwise. I set off to the surgery one Saturday morning and she thought she would treat us to scotch eggs for lunch. A nice idea, except that she managed to set fire to the deep fat pan. Fortunately, not too much damage was done, just a hole in the lino and a bit of smoke. Worse was to follow a few years later. I had left supper ready for Michael's return from work while I went down the road to my Spanish class. Maryse, our au pair was there for the children, but Michael felt he could manage to do his own chips. The story goes that he lit the gas, and left the kitchen, only for a moment. On his return, the kitchen was ablaze. He called the fire brigade while Carol managed to get out. Maryse, our au pair, had stopped to rescue Andrew from upstairs but, overcome by smoke, collapsed on the stairs. Michael just managed to grab them and take them to safety. All this time we were in our class. We heard the fire engines and they made a good topic of conversation about the *bombaderos* and where they might be going. Little did I know what was to greet me on my return home. Everything was black and the pungent smell of smoke filled the air. The smoke had reached every corner of the house, even into locked cupboards and the airing cupboard. It was not until after I had washed everything at least three times to get rid of the greasy black stains, that I realised that help could have come from the insurance company, who eventually helped us to restore cracked windows, fallen lights and redecorate the place. The smell, I shall never forget. Later that year we went on holiday to France. While we were out for the day, they had a fire in their kitchen. We returned to the smell and I found myself shaking at the memory.

Our first dog, Bobby, a Heinz 57 variety, was followed by Mahler who managed to produce eight puppies and then the gloriously beautiful Sheba; beautiful when setting out on a walk but on the return journey, passing comments were always 'ugh', after she had rolled in every muddy pool within reach. Some thought I was cruel to subject her to the hosepipe on our return, but for her part and her love of water, it was a real treat, not a punishment. Our dog-walking always took us to Greenwich Park and later to Shooter's Hill Woods, the ideal spots so close to home. Thanks to her nature and her beauty, Sheba seemed to get away with her many misdemeanors.

I recall the day I took her to Greenwich Park for a short walk before I returned to my evening surgery. On entering the park, I freed her from her lead, and she was off, over the hill and gone from sight. I traipsed through the park from one end to the other, up and down the hills calling her name. Darkness was beginning to fall and I was worried. I felt I must report her missing before I left the park. I headed for the park keepers' hut, hoping that she might have been spotted by them, but sadly no. Just as I was about to give up on my quest, a police car came down the mall and stopped by the hut. There, in the back seat of their car was my dog, looking very pleased with herself. For a moment I hesitated, concerned that if I claimed her, I might be accused of failing to control her properly. However, the decision was not in my hands; she recognised me and rushed over, wagging her tail. I feared instant arrest as the police woman approached. The tone in her voice surprised me. It was not reproachful as she said, 'What a beautiful dog, and so obedient. We say sit and she sits!' It appeared that she had got out of the park and run across the road in front of a woman who had collected her two children from school. The woman had taken pity on her, put her in the car and driven home. She had found my telephone number on her collar, but when she tried to phone I, of course, was not there. Not knowing what to do, she had then taken Sheba to the police station who had then brought her back to the park at that very moment. As I drove home, the words, 'What a beautiful dog, and so obedient,' kept ringing in my ears. I was not quite so sure.

Holidays were also included and over the years we managed trips to Spain, Mallorca, France and Crete where sun and sea allowed us to relax, bathe and recharge our batteries, while the children built sandcastles, scoured the pools for crabs and learned to swim in the sea and swimming pools.

As time went on Michael's job moved down to Margate where he spent most of the week. Weekends frequently involved golf for him and other outings, while the children got more involved with their particular interests, Jan going far with her gymnastics with Mrs Prestige down at Ladywell, Carol joining a band of young ones with her clarinet and Andrew, much to my concern, desperate for and finally acquiring a motor scooter.

By about 1968, my father had retired, but sadly could not enjoy the retirement to which he had looked forward. Shortly after his last day at work he suffered a heart attack, which after a cardiac arrest, left him partially disabled in body, but not in spirit. Since his childhood experiences in the New Forest, this had always held a special place in his heart. My parents decided to take a few breaks in the Forest Park Hotel at Brockenhurst. They chose a room on the ground floor looking out on to the garden. We, with the children, joined them on a number of occasions and he gained much pleasure from watching their antics and efforts in the pool. Meals were taken together. We were waited on by Basil always with his fund of jokes such as, 'What did the grape say when the elephant sat on it?' Response, 'It didn't say anything, it just let out a little wine'. It was this exposure to the forest scene that led us to think of acquiring a holiday home in the area. Michael did the rounds and came up with the perfect answer, the bungalow in Copse Road in Burley. We tried to get down for weekends and holidays as often as possible and when the children's other commitments permitted. They, and the dogs, loved the freedom of the country and we had the added advantage that my sister-in-law lived not so far away in Portsmouth. She together with her brood, Margaret, Richard and David, as well as our Jenny became frequent visitors during our stays in the cottage and the game of golf was added to our activities.

Burley had a lot going for it, so much so that Michael felt that we should do up the cottage so that it would be suitable for retirement. For the first time in a long while, I felt that at last he was working towards a future for us together. I threw myself into the project with gusto and when all was completed, in the summer of 1984, we held a party for all those in the village who had made us so welcome, and to say that we were here and wanted to stay. I was on a high. It seemed unbelievable when, within about two weeks I returned home one evening to find a note saying that he had left me and, after twenty-nine years of marriage, would not be coming back.

CHAPTER 9

The children (1958 to present time)

THERE CAN BE NO DOUBT THAT the arrival of children in the family changes life forever. Never again can one consider any activity without first ensuring that the children are catered for. A wealth of books on pregnancy and child-rearing cannot prepare one for the responsibility and the feeling of panic when one arrives home with the first-born. I crossed the threshold with Janet in my arms, realising that the next feed was looming and I was on my own. Never in my life have I been so glad to see the health visitor at the door. One starts with all sorts of ideals about the bringing up of children. In the 1950s, Dr Spock's book was the expert opinion on how it should be done. It is easy to look back fifty years later and have learned that most children survive in spite of us. When my daughter was born, mixed feeding at an early age was the rage; it was almost a case of steak and chips from the first week of life. Now, hands are raised in horror if anything other than milk passes their lips, for the first six months. All I can say is that all my three children, the nine grandchildren and two great-grandchildren have thrived whichever method has been tried.

The other thing not dealt with in the books is, how to deal with sleep deprivation. After weeks of disturbed nights, four-hourly feeds and pitiful crying, one just longs for the luxury of a full night's sleep. A busy routine during the day of washing and changing nappies, sterilising bottles, feeding, together with the fun time of play with the new arrival, leaves little enough time for the preparation of meals, shopping and the routine housework, let alone the opportunity to catch up on sleep. It is a hard time for all, including one's husband and other children as they come along. There were about four years between each of my children, enough for the older ones to be 'helpful', but also old enough to interfere with one's idealistic rules of training children. By the time Andrew arrived, it was impossible to put my foot down. They either laughed at his antics or thought I was being unkind; either way he thought he was on a winner. However, once again deviation from the rules has not ended in

43

disaster. I now have three grown, adult children who are all parents themselves, and are making a very good job of it. One thing that never fails to surprise me is the fact that they seem to apply the same code of living to their own children, in spite of the fact that they often objected to that same system in their own childhood. There is common ground too, in the celebration of birthdays and Christmas in exactly the same way that we did in their youth, with the decorating of the Christmas tree, Father Christmas, the hanging out of stockings at Christmas time and the blowing out of candles and the singing of 'Happy Birthday' while we cut the cake as each child achieves another year.

My memories of their childhood do not necessarily match with theirs. In talking to them now, they recall a very happy childhood in which their father played an important part. He was the one that first let go of my daughter's bike, leaving with her the vivid memory of the first time she had ridden unaided. The fun of helping him with work on the vegetable patch is a common theme to all of them and my son enjoyed his initiation into golf at Michael's golf club at Sundridge Park, and also at Burley. Each of them developed a great fondness for my parents, where there was always an open door and special treats in family get-togethers and when a baby sitter was required. Even today they feel there is something special about having sliced sausage and beetroot for breakfast, as well as a prize for being good.

Now, they look back at long hot summers, playing in the garden, splashing in the paddling pool, tea parties in the summer-house, swinging high on the swing, making camps under the table and playing in the tree-house next door. As they grew older they developed their own friends. 'Scatty' Ann near our house in Abergeldie Road, Lee and later, Annabel, across the road and Noelle a school friend, were Jan's particular companions. Carol palled up with Wendy from school, and Andrew made a constant companion of Richard. Each also had their own particular interests. Janet became a regular attender at the Ladywell Centre in Lewisham, where Mrs Prestidge, an England coach, encouraged them to do great things. For three years running in the early 1970s Janet achieved medals in the British Team Championships in gymnastics at Billingham: two gold medals and one silver. All, including Mrs Prestidge, worked hard for this title; she was a remarkable woman who could cope with a class of up to 100 excitable children, just released from a day at school, without the need ever to raise her voice. Her reward was great dedication to the sport, great respect from her pupils and the ability to draw the best out of each and every one.

Carol was helped by another dedicated and talented person, John. Having taught herself to play the recorder, she chose to take up the clarinet. Fred, a musician in the orchestra at the Covent Garden Opera House, agreed to give her lessons. She took to it straight away, just at the moment when John was setting up a small band for beginners. The players in the band were a mixture of normal and mentally and/or physically disabled children. With great patience he prepared them to perform in public, sometimes having to teach them how to play a note, before the sound could be put together. The result was remarkable and resulted in a number of concerts put on to entertain us and the public. Carol seemed to enjoy performing and glowed in the unforgettable performance as the front of the horse in the pantomime, *Dick Turpin*, put on by the Brownies. All went well until they left the stage for a few moments rest. It was hot in the horse disguise, so she and her friend took advantage of the break to come up for air. Unbeknownst to them, in their haste to return to the stage, the costume became twisted in the middle, much to the amusement of the audience who reacted with hysterical laughter, while Carol and her friend at the rear, were oblivious as to why they were causing such amusement. Dressing up was obviously her forte. Fancy dress parties are always a bit of an effort for the parents but sometimes it is the simplest of ideas that wins the show. Carol went to the school fancy dress party as a schoolboy. She was nine and went clothed in her five-year old brother's uniform several sizes too small. Shirt buttons did not do up, jacket sleeves were too short, trousers did not meet in the middle and socks crumpled to half mast. Carol carried the whole thing off to win first prize. She glowed on her return home. Later Carol became a cadet in a St John's Ambulance group in Eltham run by a Mrs Gilbert. I was also taken on as Medical Officer for the group and had to take the exams there. Later I was promoted to the title of Serving Sister of the Order of St John.

One yearly occasion in which they all took part was the Contact Christmas Party. A friend of mine organised a group in our area. Life for the housebound can, so easily, become monotonous, lonely and boring. People were recommended to join the group by Social Services and other contacts. Every month, each volunteer would pick up their particular nominated friend and drive them into the country for tea, at the home of a volunteer hostess. A beautiful spread of sandwiches, scones and cakes was always laid on and much appreciated by all. The Christmas outing was held at our house; the guests included our housebound friends, ourselves and also all our families. One of the nice things about this event was that, the 'helped' did not look upon it as charity. They felt that the helpers enjoyed the outings as much as they did, and the getting to know our partners and children was an added bonus. I recall the day when I was down in the New Forest. It was Contact day and I felt I could not let down my particular charge. I only just made it back to London in time to pick her up. As she greeted me she remarked, 'I really felt I did not want to go today – but I know that you enjoy it so much!' Just as it should be, I felt.

Time passed and schooldays were nearly over. The teens may be an exciting and fun time for the young but for parents it can be a rather traumatic period. Naturally you want the best for your children and wrong decisions at this stage of life can be seen by the older generation as a threat to the rest of their lives. Certainly, for me this was the case. All three of them did well in achieving O levels. Janet's academic prowess had always overshadowed any potential in the artistic field. When it came to her A levels she took four subjects, adding on an extra exam in mathematics, just for fun. She did well in all her subjects and from her own choosing, elected to study medicine. She was accepted as a student at the Royal Free Medical School and spent the first year there before she opted out. Things had not been easy for her. She had moved into a flat, close to the Medical School. Within a short space of time, there was a fire in the building, quite a frightening experience, and one which meant that she must find alternative accommodation. She found a flat in Tufnell Park. The house was shared by others, and in the upstairs flat lived Greg. Greg had been a student at the London College of Music and saw his future in the music trade as a guitarist. With my background, art and music were considered to be a nice hobby, but to earn a living, it was necessary to do a 'proper job'. The fact that Jan and Greg got

1. James King (my great-great-grandfather) Grandpa Watkins' grandfather

2. James Valentine Watkins (my great-grandfather) Grandpa Watkins' father

3. Ellen Eliza Watkins née King (my great-grandmother) Grandpa Watkins' mother

4. Steven Jones (my great-grandfather) Grandad Jones' father – with Matilda Homer and family

5. Catharine Batten (my great-grandmother) Grandma Jones' mother

6. Catharine Batten with all her girls in the cart

7. A Watkins family wedding about 1905 – my grandfather's sister's wedding

8. The Finch family – Granny Watkins with her parents and family

9. Emily Alice Watkins née Finch – my Granny Watkins

10. George Watkins – my Grandpa Watkins

11. William and Helen Jones – née Batten – my Grandma and Grandad Jones,
my mother's side and Dorothy (my mother's sister)

12. *Frank Watkins – my father as a boy*

13. *Margaret and Dorothy Jones – my mother and her sister*

14. *Margaret Watkins née Jones – my mother*

15. *Frank Watkins – my father*

close, filled me with some alarm, especially when Janet decided to leave college and take off for a trip round America. After six months she returned and got herself into University College Hospital to train as a nurse with an SRN qualification.

Janet and Greg married a few months later, with Greg assuring me that he would make his future living entirely by playing his guitar. Mothers do not always know best. Greg has not only made his living with his guitar, but done a great deal better than any of us. Every year we go to London to hear him play at the Pizza Express in Dean Street. We and the rest of the audience are captured by the sounds of the 'smooth jazz' that emanates from his guitar, with music that he and his working partner have written together. Over the years, they have produced many, very successful albums under the title of Acoustic Alchemy. Apart from being successful, he is a delightful person and Janet obviously knew what she was doing when she took him on.

I was wrong about Jan too. Her academic ability was only a part of her skills. Once the children had arrived, she took herself off for a City and Guilds Diploma in toy-making, creating the most delightful and entertaining toys. In particular she excels in the field of things for dolls' houses, plates of food, tiny boxes, collections of minute shells and small boxes full of the necessary for artists. As well as all this she has brought up three lovely children and personally restored much of their now very beautiful home. Nicola, Louise and Penny have now moved on to live great lives. Nicola's passion in life has been skating. Since leaving school she has worked at the local ice rink where she coaches on the ice and also in the gym there. Several times she has taken off and performed in ice shows on the Continent and is now getting just as keen on her dancing. Currently she is thinking of settling for a more conventional way of life and going into teaching. Louise, having graduated at college is on the managerial side and making waves at Top Shop. Penny has done two years of chemistry at Bristol University and is now in the States for a year working in research before she returns to finish her degree. Jan and Greg can only be described as happy, and I am happy for them.

At the time when we were beginning to think about Carol's future, plans were suddenly halted by the discovery that she was pregnant. Both she and her boy friend, Guy, were delighted at the news, married shortly after and both stayed with us until they found and could afford to buy a home of their own in Gillingham. Joanna duly arrived on 31 August 1980 and quickly won our hearts. There might be the feeling that motherhood had come to my daughter a bit too soon, but on the other hand I feel that I have been so lucky to be young with my grandchildren, play with them and really get to know them. A few years later, Guy left the police force and they moved down to Brighton where they ran a fish and chip shop. It was a busy and exacting life that took its toll, but Carol, always one to make the best of things, coped well and produced the most delicious fish and chips, as well as Mars Bars in batter. Sadly, by the time Joanna reached her teens, Carol and Guy split up. Carol then embarked on a new life in the business world of computing. She got a job as an assistant in a solicitor's office where she learned her skills in computing. Since that time, her life has taken a new turn. Now she is a director in a company of commercial estate agents, in charge of the technology throughout the firm, happily remarried to Neil and rearing my two, delightful new grandchildren Daniel and Sophie. Joanna is now married to Andy and more than busy with her two children Henry and Ruby. However, she is now managing to take a correspondence course in writing. Already we are seeing some exciting stories.

Next came my son, Andrew. Never has he been the one to conform. I well remember the day I attended the school Open Day to watch him in the trial for the rugby team, in which he did not wish to be included. He played, but with minimum effort, thus ensuring that he was not included amongst the elite team members. As he said, he did not want to give up his free time at home, to play in matches. When it came to O levels, he worked hard and did well, but once embarked on the A level course, he decided that it was time to leave and move on. The trouble was that he did not know what he wanted to move on to. I took him to a firm of career analysts. He cooperated well with their programme and they produced an excellent report, with graphs to demonstrate his strengths and weaknesses. I think the most pertinent remark came as a PS at the end: 'Andrew will be very good at selling things to people who don't want to buy'. They had summed him up perfectly. Andrew is a people's person. He has unlimited friends and would always give them his last halfpenny or do anything for them, and that includes me. Equally, if he is in need or wishes to borrow something, there are always half a dozen of the said items on the doorstep when he arrives home. I cannot say that I didn't find his teenage years difficult. He developed a love of music, especially, if it was loud, and he was really into scooters. I spent many a sleepless night waiting for the sound of his engine chugging up the hill, announcing his safe arrival home. Scooters, to me, were dangerous and perhaps not without reason. Andrew lost at least one friend and another seriously injured, because of them. Time passes and life is taken more seriously. The arrival of Lee, my grandson, opened his eyes and has been really good for all of us. After a number of years 'cabbing' in Blackheath, he has now developed a business selling old vinyl records from the last sixty years on the internet. He loves the job, has his fill of music and has time to spare for his new, growing family. Andrew and Breda married in 2002. It is a very happy home with lots of laughter, as well as my other two lovely, very lively grandchildren James and Rose. Lee travels up to London daily to work in a company that deals with patents. He is a sticker and very loyal having been in the same job for several years.

CHAPTER 10

Years of practice (1958–90)

I WAS MARRIED AND WITH MY new daughter Janet, just a few months old. We had moved to a beautiful house, Martins, in Willow Grove, Chislehurst, next door to some wonderful neighbours, Margaret and Charles Foster and their two young children, Jane and Sarah. Everything in the garden should have been great, but I soon realised that, come what may, I would have to work.

The idea was not entirely alien to me. I was a qualified doctor, had served my time in the necessary house jobs allowing me to be fully registered with the General Medical Council, and so was in the position of being able to choose in what direction I would head. I had worked hard for this position and it did seem a shame to allow it all to go to waste. However, a hospital job, with the requirement to 'live in', was out of the question with a home to run and a young babe to care for. General practice seemed to be the answer and so it was with gratitude that I accepted the offer of a job as a trainee in general practice, down the road at St Paul's Cray.

The practice was an interesting one, coping largely with patients living on the relatively new council estate. The five partners in the practice, each with their own particular interests and expertise, gave me wide experience in family care, not only in medicine and the patients' needs, but also in hypnosis. They were an innovative practice, always ready to accept new ideas and put them into practice. There was also the encouragement to attend courses and lectures, so important if one is to keep up with all the latest developments in medicine. Back in 1959, when I took this job, it was not necessary to go through a training year; so there was no bar to launching straight into practice. For me, the year was invaluable. One leaves hospital medicine thinking one knows it all, but dealing with families, at home, with diseases that never reach the hospital gates, and sometimes in less than ideal conditions, is a completely different ball game, requiring different skills and a lot of common sense. There is nothing like doing a visit in the middle of the night, on one's own and having to take decisions without resource to a second opinion or the immediate back up of hospital facilities.

My next move was to a practice in Downham, Kent in 1960. The senior partner, a Dr Mizen, was about to retire and a new assistant was required to fill the gap. Fortunately for me it was suggested that I covered the last two months of her time, in order to get to know the practice and its ways, before taking over with the remaining partner, Dr Joan Latham. I was supposed to live on the job and we moved into a house at 102 Kidbrooke Park Road, a few doors along from Dr Mizen, so that I could continue the Blackheath end of the practice from there.

I have to say that it was with some reluctance that I took the job. Jan was now a toddler, great fun and needing more of my time. However, needs must and we took on a housekeeper with a young son, to cope with the home care. Dr Mizen retired on 30 September 1959. I went to bed that night with just one prayer in my mind: for some miracle to prevent me from taking over the next day. Sometimes miracles do happen. My prayers were answered. I woke the next morning with chickenpox! With relief I called my new boss who was not all that sympathetic. Her response was, 'When I had the mumps, I worked right through it!' I managed to see a few patients that morning in the home surgery before thankfully taking to my bed with a high fever, and a blissful two to three weeks off sick. At the end of that time, the return to work did not seem quite so daunting.

General practice in those days was different from that which we experience today. The practice in Downham was run from two premises, apart from the Blackheath end. There was the main surgery at 2 Oakshade Road, manned by a nurse who organised things, took out of hours calls and lived above 'the shop'. A second lock-up surgery was in the shopping area on Bromley Hill, above the launderette. When I first started there, no notes were kept at this second surgery, no question of ever getting a chaperone, no paper towels and syringes, and instruments were recycled through a bit of spirit in a bowl. I hate to think what Health and Safety would have thought of that, but of course, in those days we did not have the problems of MRSA. With some opposition, the notes situation was changed and I dared to start an appointments system, much against my partner's better judgement. However, to her surprise, she had to admit, a few weeks later, that not only did the new system work but it had revolutionised life in the surgery.

After my year as an Assistant, things went on hold and another young woman was employed in my place. We moved to 57 Abergeldie Road, Lee. Carol was on the way and I was able to do just a few sessions in the practice. Andrew was born four years later in 1966 and after his birth, I was recruited back into the practice as a third part-time partner. Three of us then did the work of two; a very satisfactory arrangement.

Medicine has changed a lot since those days. I was on the obstetric list, of which home deliveries were a part. I was never particularly happy with babes being born at home, but the local policy was to book for hospital care only first pregnancies and those who developed problems or had had previous problems with births. We took particular care to book only those about whom we felt confident; however, nature does not always cooperate and the unforeseen crisis at home is always a nightmare. In spite of all our precautions we were faced with worrying complications on several occasions, the flying squad had to be called and the consultant involved finally changed his policy on home bookings, much to my relief.

The other thing that still never fails to surprise me is that medicines which we considered to be essential to treatment in those days are now thought to be unnecessary or even frowned upon. Both treatments and diseases have changed over the years. Some, such as measles, we now rarely see since the introduction of the MMR vaccine in 1988, but the 1980s saw the advent of AIDS with all its potentially disastrous results. Initially there was no 'cure' but thankfully today, drugs are available that do seem to contain the problem in countries where it can be afforded. It always seems that there is something new about which to worry. MRSA and the need for meticulous hygiene is currently high on the agenda and concerns about the new swine flu have hit the headlines in the last year (2009).

The media have been responsible for creating a number of hysterical reactions to fears. Yes, it is important to quickly alert patients and medical personnel about anxieties, but sometimes this information is detrimental, as in the case of the pill scare in 1995. By the time more research that refuted the claims, came out four years later, many had discontinued their pill, achieved an unwanted pregnancy and felt the need to undergo a termination, with all its attendant risks. At least now there is choice about abortion, but until the Act of 1967 a medical abortion could be performed only to save a woman's life. Those that resorted to an illegal abortion were often risking a fatal outcome.

For better or worse, things are very different today. Computers are supposed to have replaced some of our role. They tell us that computer diagnosis and the opportunity to look up the latest management should make life easy. Now, doctors no longer have the freedom to practise their art without referral to guidelines and evidence-based medicine. All the time one risks legal action if things do not work out, a system that makes it very difficult to practise good medicine without a host of investigations that are often actually unnecessary. Fine, statistics do prove something, but they do not take into consideration the differences in the patients who are to be treated. No two people, or their circumstances, are ever the same. Computers may be a guide but while we are so busy on the machines, we should not forget to actually look at our patients and glean those non-verbal signs that so often lead us into the real problem from which the patient is suffering and making them ill.

In 1974, another big change came to my life. After sixteen years at Downham, I decided to move to the Lakeside Health Centre at the growing estate on the Erith Marshes, Thamesmead. It shows how times have changed. Women doctors are now commonly employed in general practice and in medicine generally. It is only thirty-six years ago that my future senior partner, Peter Higgins, remarked at my interview, 'I always thought there might be a place for a woman in General Practice.'

Thamesmead was a most stimulating experience, not only in the field of medicine, but also as a community and in architectural design. The site of this new town was the marshland outside Woolwich. This land had to be drained before building work could start and in achieving this, some attractive lakes were formed. Flooding was always considered to be a risk from the outset, so the first two stages of the development were built on stilts. Houses, tower blocks and maisonettes as well as the Health Centre were all entered at first floor level, via bridged walkways. Ground level was reserved for car parking and garages. The area was often of interest to groups of architects who visited from many distant parts of the world. Unfortunately, the building of the Thames Barrier, opened in 1984 and said to be the eighth wonder of the world, has not changed the flood risk in this area.

The plan was to re-house the many who were seeking accommodation from the Greater London area. The first tenants moved there in 1968. We finished up with a largely young community from various parts of London, including the East End. Many were English and used to our ways but there was also a large number of foreign origin, including a number of Vietnamese boat people, following the fall of Saigon in 1975. In fact, while I was there we served as many as thirty-three different nationalities. Newcomers to the estate, uprooted from their supports of family and friends, had the benefit of a modern new home of their own but without the security of Mum or Grandma round the corner to run to in time of trouble. Consequently, the Health Centre was so often their first port of call.

When I first went to work there, we were fortunate to have Jim Thompson (later Bishop of Bath and Wells) as the local vicar. He was a very practical man who had gone into the Church after a career as an accountant. He made himself available to all, churchgoers and non-religious alike. He started the practice of knocking on the door of every new arrival, in order to introduce himself and to offer help and support should it be required. He also knocked on the door of the Health Centre and worked very closely with us. Like us, he soon appreciated the large numbers of people on the estate with problems of one kind or another; people whose lives were in chaos through marriage breakdown, illness, bereavement, unemployment, financial difficulties or their children. He realised that these distressed individuals were seeking help but often through many different doors, thus frequently receiving conflicting advice. He had the idea of centralising care using the Health Centre as a base to which patients could come without displaying to all the fact that they were not coping with life. First he started a discussion group amongst us workers to talk about the situation and pool our ideas and experiences. The group comprised doctors, nurses, social workers, probation officer, clergy and psychiatric nurse. After a year, a group of counsellors volunteered from this group to set up at the Health Centre, a service to which those in need could be referred. Here was a non-threatening centre with the offer of a choice of worker for counselling and support through their difficulties. We also had the benefit of contact with the other workers at times when we needed to debrief, to learn from their experiences and to enlist their help in a situation when joint counselling was required with both a male and female worker. We called the group MASH (Marriage and Self Help) and functioned at a time when workers were prepared to give their services free to such a cause. When Jim left, I continued to run the group for another thirteen years until I left in 1990.

Not long after I started work at Thamesmead, Peter Higgins, our senior partner, was appointed as Professor of General Practice at Guy's Hospital. With this link, the rest of the partners, five in number, were enlisted to the staff of the department at Registrar grade and so were involved in the teaching of medical students. It was a time when the policy was to introduce students, early in their training, for exposure to real patients and general practice. Groups in their first year would come down to us for their first (volunteer) patient contact, to take a medical history, find out more about the individual and how this information could affect their management. The emphasis was always on the 'whole' patient in medical, psychological and social terms, and to encourage patients to talk of their previous experiences, good and bad, with the medical profession so that they could understand the various influences that affect patient care. A second placement was arranged for students later in their training in which they dealt with patients directly, under our supervision. Thamesmead was a teaching practice, not only for students, but also for GPs in training, known then as Trainees (now Registrars). By 1978, I was designated a Trainer and did the necessary Trainer's course before taking on a number of Trainees myself.

At this point I felt the need to have some qualification that might back my ability to take on this job. Consequently I took the examination for the Membership of the Royal College of General Practitioners (MRCGP). To my relief, I passed, in spite of the traumas associated with the multiple choice questionnaire. This involved 100 questions which required a simple yes or no answer. Every GP knows that it is never possible to be so decisive; always, it seems the answer must be 'yes, if . . .' or 'no, but . . .' Each correct answer was to be allotted one point. For each wrong answer a point was to be deducted. Fifty points were required for a pass. I decided to answer fifty that I knew to be correct and forget the rest. Sadly, my certainties numbered forty-nine only! The trouble then started as I struggled to achieve the pass mark. From then, I resolved never again to take another exam, and thank goodness, there has never been the need.

Thamesmead was a great place to work and one felt privileged to be there. We met with those from all walks of life, in a society that comprised almost exclusively Classes 3, 4 and 5 – if one is allowed to speak of class. Many had led tough lives, some had survived broken homes and/or disability, some were illiterate through no fault of their own, but due to lack of education during the war, others were involved with crime and had served time in prison. All had a story to tell that helped us to understand the situations in which they now found themselves. One great advantage of working on the estate was the fact that, on the several occasions that I managed to lock my car keys inside the car, the next passer-by was always able to come to my rescue, gain access and retrieve the keys for me within minutes. I recall a nun who was head teacher of one of the schools on the estate. She was a lovely, dedicated woman, calm and serene. I asked her, 'How do you cope with all the problems that come through your door?' Her response was, 'Who knows, if I had been through their experiences, what I would have done?' A humbling thought.

During my years at Thamesmead we went through some exciting moments. Life was never dull. One Thursday afternoon we were interrupted by a frantic man at our door, shouting for help. His wife 'was on the bridge and just had the baby.' We, myself and the health visitor, rushed to the scene, to find the patient lying on the stone pathway with the new baby, next to a large man waving a machete, 'ready to cut the cord'. We were able to save him the trouble and get the girl to hospital.

A week later, the whole of Thamesmead was cleaned up and uplifted in a visit by Queen Elizabeth and Prince Philip. They wanted to see us at work during a 'normal' surgery. This was difficult to achieve, in a situation when no one was allowed to enter or leave the building for an hour before her arrival and the building had been taken over and searched by police for the previous twenty-four hours. The moment arrived. Philip marched up to the reception desk and asked, 'Where can I get an aspirin?' The Queen included my room in her visit and spoke to an elderly patient brought in for the occasion, together with her carer and a nurse. I was lucky, as the press were not allowed to follow her around the building, so I was delegated to take photographs in the inner sanctum. It was amazing how this often denigrated town was boosted by the 1980 visit that hit the headlines.

Psychiatric problems were always a nightmare. I recall one fateful morning when I was called early to a woman in a state of high agitation, with paranoia. She was not actually our patient, but visiting relatives on the estate. Consequently our local psychiatric hospital refused to get involved and no ambulance was prepared to take her back to her home in north London. I battled on the phone for what seemed like hours in trying to find some solution to the problem, while the disturbed patient seemed to take delight in hitting me over the head! Eventually the police came to the rescue. I returned to the surgery over an hour late, only to find all the fully booked list of patients had chosen to await my arrival; quite hard to cope with.

Night visits were the other challenge. Come rain, hail or snow for much of my time in post, we did our own night work. We did have the advantage of knowing the patients and knowing our way around, but wandering around the estate at midnight, to homes that were approached via underground garages and parking lots, and/or lifts in tower blocks was somewhat daunting. I am not brave. Sleep deprivation also took its toll. The working day was long and exacting and not conducive to enjoyment of disturbed nights, especially when one was expected to function normally the next day. Somehow we coped, but when my first retirement came, I vowed that, if I ever worked again, I would never do out of hours work at night or weekends.

All good things come to an end. The Government was stepping in and beginning to change the approach to general practice in their *Health of the Nation* Green Paper of 1991. I foresaw the extra work that would be involved to meet with directives and the fact that by the time things should have calmed and changes implemented, I would be due for retirement anyway. It was sad to see ministers devaluing our work, suggesting that we were interested only in the money in our pocket, something that had only rarely been the case until that time. I myself felt that I would no longer be able to treat patients in the way that they deserved. It was also a milestone in my life. Michael had gone for good, the divorce was through and the time had come for me to resign from Thamesmead and start a new life in the New Forest at Burley. Thamesmead workers and patients gave me a great send off.

For my farewell, I decided not to do a speech but to offer up a poem. It went as follows:

A Tribute to Lakeside Friends and Thamesmead

It's sixteen years since I came here, with doubts of trying something new,
I well remember that first day when Peter led my interview.
The questions flew around the room, at first they seemed unsure
Could I cope with all the work, could I the stress endure?

The thing that seemed to sway their votes was when they asked if I kept notes.
'Of course', I said, 'but just one problem. Having made them, can you read them?'
Peter's manner quickly changed.
My new appointment was arranged.

I started with some trepidation. Life was very different here
I felt strange in this new setting. People spotted my inner fear.
Cups of tea just kept appearing, when I needed them the most
Others asked me round at lunchtime. Thamesmead was a friendly place.

The work is hard, the day is long. Our patients to the door do throng
Our cars are under constant threat, missiles aimed at us too – and yet
We stay to man the fort for years. When parting comes, it's time for tears
This place is warm, the friendship strong. What fun we've had through all the years.

The memories come flooding in. With Betty armed with sheet and pin
And us in tow across the street, not sure of what we were to meet
There, sure enough, our patient lay, delivered of a baby boy
A butcher's knife to cut the cord. The mum lay there without a word.

Next week the Queen to visit us. This all created quite a fuss
Some weeks were spent in preparation, with paint and brush for
    redecoration
Alas, that now, when sorely needed, our cries for more, fail to be
    heeded.
There's no more money for our ceiling, with paint and plasters badly
    peeling.

Cooperation twixt different workers, has been the greatest thing for
    me.
In MASH, First Aid Groups and the Nameless, memories will always
    be
Of privilege to work with others, learn from them and make new
    friends
Finding that, with all our efforts, we can achieve a common end.

Nothing can replace the laughter of the day we met to learn,
about first aid for pregnant mothers. Suddenly, June had a turn
Quickly, Mary to the rescue, competent midwife of the past
June lay groaning on the hard floor, delivered of her 'doll' at last.

It's times like this that I'll remember. Times when all, with one accord
Get together, plan and muster, parties that are quite superb.
It is then that the great spirit of Lakeside inmates come to the fore
Preparation, eating, drinking, even washing up's no chore.

Fun and friendship, they have kept me, here at Thamesmead up till
    now
Through those times when life was painful, boosted me when I was
    low
Friendship of the Thamesmead workers is the thing I value most
Friendship too of all my patients. To them I'd like to give a toast.

Now I'm moving to the country, please remember that I'm there
Keep in contact, come and see me, it's not so far for you to go.
I must thank you all at Thamesmead, for sixteen memorable years
It's been great. I won't forget it. I really feel it's worth three cheers.

CHAPTER 11

The turning point (1978)

IT SEEMS INCREDIBLE THAT JUST one unplanned and unexpected moment can change the rest of your life. I was forty-eight, married with three growing children, still set on somehow making a success of the marriage. My thoughts centred around the family and my job, and the fact that, at home we could enjoy family things that included holidays. For ten years I had saved in a regular savings plan so that we might all manage to take a break in Australia to visit the other half of our family, the Beans. My Aunt Nell, Uncle David, David, James and Andrew had all managed to keep in touch, by relatively regular visits and years in college in the UK. It was time for us make a return visit now that they had settled 'down under', in Sydney. The savings plan matured and I was ready to take the holiday with the family. Sadly, Michael's response to the suggestion was, 'I don't want to go'. A heavy gloom sank over me. When I think of what I have done since, it seems ridiculous, but the thought of going on my own never crossed my mind. Such an adventure was out of the question alone. I did not have the confidence to make the journey by myself and, in any case, part of the pleasure of doing things is to be able to share experiences.

It was on one Saturday morning that I was sitting on the bed, turning the pages of the *British Medical Journal* (BMJ). It fell open at a page on which there was an advertisement for a 'Medical Study Tour of China'. Never in my wildest dreams had I ever thought of embarking on such an adventure. In my depressed state, I heard myself saying, 'How would you like me to go to China?' Michael's response was one of complete lack of interest as he said, 'OK'. My instant reaction was, 'I'm going'. Our friend Jenny was delighted to move in and cope with the children and they were more than happy to be with her. Thus, I booked for the trip that was to completely change the course of the rest of my life.

The tour was organised by a GP, Peb Brown, from Kent who had managed to visit the country a couple of times before. Our group of sixteen was an interesting mix. It comprised other GPs, a consultant gynaecologist and his wife, nurses, some professional photographers, a minister of religion who was researching the state of the Church in China, and the current medical correspondent of the *Telegraph*, David Loshak.

The year 1978 was an interesting time to visit this country. Mao had died two years earlier and the country was emerging from a regime that had left an estimated 50–70 million people dead, millions banished to the country to work on the fields, and the majority of the population were living in communes from which there was little escape. Private enterprise was forbidden, there was no private motoring and the theatre was restricted to productions that supported government policies. Mao's death had led to the beginning of change. There was an enthusiasm amongst the people to work and build for a better future in the year 2000. Constantly we heard the words, 'We are working for the four modernisations', namely 'in agriculture, industry, technology and defence'. Amidst this enthusiasm there was sameness in every field, equality of pay, equality of living conditions and equality of dress. The national uniform was the Mao jacket and cap. All were employed at something, but without the luxury of mechanisation many hands were necessary to fulfill the needs. Their knowledge of anything outside their commune was grossly limited, with information fed to them by government edicts only. Knowledge outside the country was nil; on our visit to the newspaper wall in Beijing, none had ever heard of a washing machine and they knew nothing of the moon landing in 1969. It was not surprising, therefore, that our presence caused so much interest. Many had never seen a European before. Wherever we went, crowds gathered round us in the streets, to stare – then to smile, wave and then to clap.

History was in the making on our visit to Shanghai. We were caught in a traffic jam outside the old football stadium. An enormous crowd of 10 to 20,000 people had gathered to attend a meeting at a time when China had just broken its ties with Russia. The meeting was held to focus on the alternative choice of joining the West. We were spotted by some on the street next to our bus and they went through the usual pattern of staring, smiling, clapping and then, unusually, cheering. The cheers caught the attention of the crowds behind. Suddenly and if as one they turned, shouting, cheering and waving at us, just as the meeting was coming to a close; the West had arrived. Our *Telegraph* correspondent managed to reach the headlines in his paper the next day with news of this extraordinary event.

As our trip was termed a medical study tour, we had the privilege of visiting a variety of hospitals and clinics, in fact we were the first group of foreigners to be allowed inside the door of a psychiatric hospital. With bars at the windows, minimal basic facilities and the inability to afford the modern medical treatments, outdated treatments such as insulin coma therapy were still in use. Schizophrenics were routinely treated with acupuncture, with needles inserted into the back of the neck and by the side of the ears. In a country that could not afford to import drugs, this was their only option. Acupuncture was also the sole choice of anaesthesia in many surgical theatres that had no anaesthetic machines. It seemed to work. We watched from the gallery while a man walked into the theatre, laid on the bed and had needles inserted into his hands and arms before they proceeded with the removal of his thyroid. He did not bat an eyelid and was able to walk back to the ward from the theatre without assistance. The commune clinics were still serviced by barefoot doctors where traditional methods of herb treatments and acupuncture played a large part. Enforcement of the one child policy dictated that termination was the only choice for anyone who broke the rules. At the same time, in the paediatric hospital in Beijing, we saw many children with preventable conditions that were rare in the UK at that time, such as rheumatic fever, nephritis and polio. This paediatric hospital was a sad place. The chief physician was back in post but tears came to his eyes as he talked about his forced move into the country to work on the fields, in Mao's time, while his hospital failed to be properly maintained.

I returned from this trip a different person, no longer the shy, nervous creature that lacked so much in confidence. My physical fear of public speaking was banished by the fact that, on my return, everyone seemed to want to hear about the trip. I actually had something to say and I had the opportunity to do so in endless slide shows to friends, colleagues and groups. Today, slide shows play a big part of my life. Having been approved by the WI to be on their speakers' list, I am able to raise money for charity by talking to the WI and many other groups in the Dorset and Hampshire area.

Before my visit to China I had never possessed a camera, in fact I bought my first camera to go on the trip. New to the game, I had a lot to learn and did not always get it right. It was not until I was watched putting in my fourth roll of film, that someone noticed that I was not doing it correctly. All these films were blank. For twenty-four hours, I went into mourning until I then decided to make up for lost time. With a number of professional photographers on the trip, I quickly learned that if one wanted to get a good picture, one must take a lot – and I mean a lot; so that is what I did. On my return home, I looked at my pictures, many of which had been taken in the medical setting. With my new enthusiasm, I took my camera into the surgery, thinking that medical pictures taken there would be useful for the teaching of medical students and trainees. Little did I realise that this step would lead to the development of the large medical library on my shelves. Little did I realise, either, the demand that there would be for the use of these pictures in a variety of medical magazines. When it all started in 1984, I thought of it as a nine-day wonder. This nine-day wonder has lasted twenty-five years.

And finally, on our return from China, David Loshak, the medical correspondent wrote up the trip in a number of magazines. With my new confidence I thought, 'If he can do it, why can't I?' This has led to another big change in my life in writing on medical and holiday subjects. If it was not for all this, I can't imagine that I would ever have got round to writing this autobiography.

CHAPTER 12

Itchy feet (1979 to present time)

THE VISIT TO CHINA HAD opened my eyes to another world. My previous travels, good though they were, had been limited to family holidays in France, Spain or England, apart from one trip to America to see our great friends and ex-neighbours, the Rays in Lexington, Virginia and on their island (Snake Island), one of the Thousand Islands on the St Lawrence River between USA and Canada. On this trip, we were also able to spend time with an old college friend of mine, Nora Spens in Stonnington, Connecticut. A superb time was had by all and enabled by a fortuitous win by Michael in the office lottery sweepstake.

I had had a slight taste for the possibility of travel in 1951 when, together with three college friends, we took our bikes to Holland for a fortnight's holiday around the country, at a time when it was recovering from the ravages of war, and the Dutch could not do enough for the British. The sum of £19 covered our boat fare, youth hostel stays, food and a few presents to take home. It shows how much inflation has affected prices. A second opportunity arose about the same time, when my father had to go to Libya to tender for a job. In the days long before Gaddafi, we toured the *souks* of Tripoli, crossed the desert and visited unspoiled, newly discovered Roman remains. Malta was a convenient stop on the way back. At that stage tourism was unthought of. We circled the island in bumpy buses and had the fascinating historical sites to ourselves.

Travel may seem an indulgent luxury. For me, these indulgencies have included visits to famous sites such as the Taj Mahal in India, the Great Wall of China, Angkor Wat in Cambodia, the Cu Chi tunnels of Vietnam and the mausoleums of famous leaders such as Eva Peron in Buenos Aires, Argentina, Mao Zedong in China and Ho Chi Minh in Vietnam. Special thrills are also attached to certain experiences such as the singing of 'Away in a Manger' in the cave (not the stable) in Bethlehem in which Jesus was born. However, travel has also helped me in my work, to appreciate the lives and cultures of many of my patients and to begin to understand the problems they must face in trying to learn our language and adapt to our ways. I had left China with its apparently ordered, progressive policies and optimistic outlook, wondering how India would compare. The opportunity to find out came a couple of years later. This time Michael was keen to come along. I found my first visit to this place difficult. I did not like what the poverty, squalor and begging did to me. One continually wonders what could be done to improve the lot of the people who live there. We were there, in the streets surrounded by the needy. Some had even been deliberately maimed in order to gain more sympathy in their quest for help. They clung to us, pleading. I felt ashamed as I brushed them off like flies, with the thought, 'One cannot help them all and to give to one is just encouraging more to cluster round.'

The chance to do something actually occurred early in the trip. Michael and I were packed up and ready to fly off to our next destination, Delhi. We had a half hour to spare and so headed off on our own, across the wasteland opposite the hotel. From the top of the hill we could see a shabby-looking shack settlement, down on the shore by the sea. As we paused to view the scene, an elderly woman appeared carrying a basket of washing on her head. She squatted on the ground near us. I thought, 'Oh Dear! Another beggar,' and tried to press a few coins into her hand. To my surprise she refused to accept them. By this time we had been spotted by the village. A young girl was running towards us. There was no escape as she pleaded, 'What can you do to help my baby?' She led us back to her home; a small poorly constructed shell of cardboard, wood and corrugated iron. There on the mud floor lay a three-month old child with severe club feet. What could we do? We offered the few coins that we had carried with us saying, 'I'm terribly sorry but we have to go and catch our plane'. Never before, or since, have I felt so bad in all my life. This shame stayed with me for the rest of the trip.

The answer came after we returned home. I had worked with a Catholic priest on Thamesmead and as we talked, I repeated my story and the fact that we had seen a Catholic church nearby and that the settlement bore a cross at its approach. Once again, I have to believe in miracles. Our priest knew someone who had just returned from working in that area of Bombay (Mumbai), who was able to supply me with the name of a charity that might be able to help. I wrote explaining the problem and enclosing a roughly drawn map of the settlement and the position of the shack, together with a picture of the girl and the child. Four months later, I received a reply. They had traced Natasha and, if I sent a donation, they would ensure that it was used to her benefit. They regularly kept me informed as to how the money was used. They had managed to get free hospital care and used the money for bandages and dressings, extra milk and food supplements; eventually they were able to get the family re-housed in better accommodation.

Eight years later I went back to Mumbai. My contact arranged for me to visit Natasha in the school at which she was performing well. She was wearing heavy boots but walking so well that the school had not realised that she had a problem. For me this was a very emotional contact. No, it is impossible to help them all, but at least it should be possible to improve the life of someone, even if it is only a drop in the ocean.

Since then I have been fortunate being able to travel widely in Asia, Australasia, South America, Africa and more recently, Europe. We've seen affluence and we have seen abject poverty, as well as the cultural differences that sometimes make it all bearable. We stayed with a wealthy family, living in a large house, with four bathrooms, in Chandigarh, in the Punjabi part of India. They employed a maid, who was housed in two small rooms upstairs. She lived there with her husband and family of ten. When we shopped in the market, it was the maid who must carry the heavy groceries and other purchases. Our offer of help was spurned by our hostess who explained that the girl was grateful and only too glad to be working in that position. 'After all,' said our hostess, 'we were good in our last life and so deserve all we have now. The maid must have sinned and will gain a better place in the next life if she suffers now'. Both seemed happy with the arrangement dictated by custom and culture. In such a status quo, perhaps any attempt to change things would be disastrous and maybe end in a blood bath?

Some of the countries we have visited such as China and Vietnam seem to emerge from tyranny with renewed vigour and hope. The country that I found to be the saddest and most depressing was Cambodia, in 2003. The whole population suffered terribly through the years of Pol Pot (1975–9). Most of our guides and contacts had somehow survived through those years with untold hardship, starvation, loss of family members and ill treatment. One in 343 of the population is an amputee as the result of landmine explosions, but with little or no compensation or opportunity of work. The orphanage was full of children with no stimulation. We could see no toys in the building and the home was finding it difficult to finance sufficient food for the children, so many of whom were also HIV positive. To me, the worst of all was the fact that many appeared to be unhappy with the current regime and what is more, would be prepared to fight to achieve change. The result would seem to be just more suffering.

Another side of our travel has given us the opportunity to view wildlife at first hand. Television brings much into our homes with its great commentaries and wonderful photography; however there is nothing, but nothing, like the opportunity to see it in real life. Surely, nothing can match the moment we reached the top of the cliff on the Valdez Peninsula in Argentina, to be greeted by the roars of two elephant seals locked in battle. An intruder had dared to encroach on the resident male's territory and harem of thirty to forty 'girls'. The ensuing bloody battle continued for over half an hour as the resident male gradually pushed the intruder back into the sea. The sea around went red as the blood flowed from the wounds. The intruder beat a retreat and flopped exhausted on the shore. One would have thought he was about to die, but no; within ten minutes he was back on his flippers and once again entering the fray. As an observer, we could also take note of the 'girls', who seemed entirely disinterested in the whole affair, as they turned away and slept.

In Amboseli National Park in Kenya we watched at the waterhole at sunset. Creatures large and small were taking their last drink of the evening. Suddenly, they all dispersed to hide behind the bushes. The reason became clear as twenty-seven elephants plodded their way across the plain. No other animal wished to be in their path. The elephants ate, bathed and drank their fill before moving on to their night-time quarters. The rest of the animals resumed their ablutions while the elephants made their way, followed by twenty-three clucking guinea fowl in their wake. An incongruous sight.

Another unforgettable moment was in the Ngala Park, adjacent to the Kruger National Park in South Africa. Our jeep drove us to an apparently empty patch of land. As we watched, the heads of twenty-two lionesses and a few lion cubs gradually appeared, peeping at us through the long grass. The male lay close by, asleep under a tree. One of the 'girls' approached him to suggest that it was time for tea. His response, although in lion language, was obviously extremely rude. The chief lioness then gathered her flock, which proceeded to circle our jeep. Our guide told us not to stand up lest they should get our scent and feel that they had an easy meal at hand. He seemed to think that as long as we remained seated that they would get the smell of oil and just see us as part of the jeep. We hoped he was right. Eventually the lions moved on for the hunt and succeeded in felling a gazelle. By this time the lord and master had stirred himself sufficiently to join them, not to assist or make the kill but to enjoy the feast. He had the first pickings, the cubs the next and the 'girls' had to make a further kill before they could satisfy their hunger; so much for equality and women's lib in the animal world.

We do not go on these holidays for adventure and danger, but somehow adventure sometimes follows us. One that quickly springs to mind is in Nepal in 1994. We had set off, before dawn, on the back of an elephant, to look for a tiger. Having endured the discomforts of the *howdah*, plunged through the river, waded through the head-high elephant grass and watched our elephant uproot a few trees that were in the way, we finished in the middle of a distinctively unattractive quagmire. I didn't know that elephants growled, but our elephant certainly did – only to be answered by another growl a few yards away. Suddenly a beautiful, sleek and shiny tiger emerged from the bushes and strolled towards the trees. We were just gathering ourselves and thinking we had been so lucky to have such a sighting when the tiger reappeared. We presumed that he was the same tiger but, with his hackles raised, he looked twice the size. Clearly he was very angry and there was no doubt that he was angry with us. He bounded up to our elephant, on the side next to me, and crouched, snarling and baring his teeth. Any thoughts of photography quickly disappeared from my mind as I attempted to move my feet out of his reach. It seemed forever before our driver (*mahout*) turned our elephant to face the tiger. The elephant lifted his trunk and let out the most almighty trumpeting sound, sufficient to scare the tiger away. As we congratulated ourselves on this amazing experience, we turned to our guide, an Indian. He was white as a sheet and trembling. He then told us what could have happened. Firstly, tigers do occasionally kill elephants, secondly if an elephant is scared, he may take off through the jungle at speed, thirdly if really frightened he will sit down. I suspect that any of these moves would not have been much help to us!

I have been so lucky to make lasting friendships with many of my fellow travellers. The nucleus of this particular group is Maggie and Jules Thompson, Betty and Ron Hoy, George and Rhoda Higgins, Norma Elsey and myself; we have been together on the majority of trips since the Ecuador experience in 1996, which was where we really bonded, although we do not always all travel together every time. We had been in the country for a few days and already found life there to be rather hazardous. Earthquakes, landslides, floods and risky driving had already led to a few near misses, several times. However, once we had reached the Amazonian jungle at Tena on the Napo River, we had hoped that things might be better. After a fairly hairy experience on the river in the morning, we were promised a gentle, two-hour walk in the jungle with one of the local Indians who would talk to us about the plants and their use in medicine. We had viewed the jungle on the previous day and I had noted in my diary, 'How great that it is still there'. By the end of our jungle walk I was not so sure about this remark.

Tropical storms are common in this area and there had been a torrential one the night before. In such conditions, the jungle paths were inevitably ill-defined, muddy and slippery, and any view obscured by a rising mist. We struggled up the first climb with some difficulty. Thoughts of turning back sounded a pleasant option but the idea of returning down the slippery slopes, edged by sheer drops, did not appeal. We soldiered on and shortly came upon a cliff of mud up which I had to be heaved. This was followed by an equally steep drop down. The only option was to sit down and slide. At the bottom we met the river over which the only way across was on a tree trunk, without handrail and just a thin piece of string by which to orientate ourselves. We made it and plodded on. Two hours stretched to three, before our guide gathered us together and in rather serious tone said, 'I think we had better hurry up as it is going to get dark and we are not yet half way'. We tried to obey instructions but shortly after, Betty fainted on the path. While we were resuscitating her, Jules came along exclaiming, 'Thank God you've stopped', clutched his chest, saying he had chest pain. Then he passed out as well. Our guides seemed to be at a loss as to what to do. Our Indian guide was the only one who knew the way back to the lodge. He, with Nick, a brave volunteer, went off to seek help. We waited as night fell. All was dark apart from the fireflies flitting between the trees. The previously silent jungle suddenly sprang to life with a cacophony of sound: roars, barks, yaps, squeaks and slithers as jungle life set out on its night's work. We waited, waited and waited . . . Eventually we heard distant voices. Nick, our guide and the local Indians from the village had come to our rescue with a few torches and Tilley lamps. They fashioned a stretcher from some tree branches and an old blanket while we formed groups and they shone the light on the path so that we might follow, down the precipitous slopes on the muddy paths until we reached lower ground. Far from this being easier, we sank into the deep mud in our Wellington boots and got stuck there. By this time we were weak and exhausted. Betty had fainted several times more, Rhoda was vomiting and Jules was humped past us in his uncomfortable stretcher before, after nine hours, we finally made it back to the road and our lodge.

This was different to our tiger experience. This was prolonged, exhausting and unpleasant, in a situation where we had no food or water to sustain us. However, we had survived and one realises that somehow, when faced with what seems to be the impossible, nature can find a way to get you through. We did feel that the Ecuadorians should have understood our age, frailty and femininity. For their part they were amazed that we had had a problem! No doubt in a country such as this, unless one can cope with this sort of situation one would not reach one's mature years. One good thing that came out of this was that the tour company feared that we would not choose to travel with them again. The following year they laid on a special tour to South Africa, just for us. Ever since it has been a case of, 'Where would you like to go?' And then, they have arranged it for us.

The experience of travel has been great for me. I have been just so lucky to have had the opportunity to make these journeys. The many experiences, both good and bad leave me with no regrets, just hoping to be able to continue for a little while yet.

CHAPTER 13

The move to Burley
(1990 to present time)

FOR AS LONG AS I CAN remember, the New Forest has figured in our family. This beautiful, largely unspoiled part of southern England lies mainly in Hampshire, between the towns of Bournemouth and Southampton. My father had happy memories of the place before the First World War of 1914. From the age of about ten, he, his sister and mother used to rent a small house in Brockenhurst for their summer holidays. They chose Brockenhurst as it was close to the railway station. My grandfather was then able to travel down to join them on a Sunday, his only day off. They grew to love the area and the country life; my father collected butterflies and my aunt built up a collection of pressed wild flowers. He talked of the fun they had 'tree bashing'; a process whereby they sampled the wild life that fell from the trees, when they hit the branches with a stick, onto a sheet placed below. 'Treacling' was another rewarding practice. After dark they would go into the forest and paint treacle on the bark of a tree, before shining lights on it to attract the local lepidopterae. Over the years he built up a fairly comprehensive collection of British butterflies and moths. Today, this would probably not have been possible without a special pass and limitations as to what, if anything, one would be allowed to collect, but at that stage in time, the expression of 'endangered species' did not seem to have reached them.

My first introduction to the forest was in 1945, at the end of World War II. In this post-war period, we came on the train, with our bikes and cycled, walked and waved our butterfly nets around, while my father reminisced about the old days. We look to the skies now and see the many planes that frequently fly overhead. My father remembers seeing his first plane flying over Beaulieu in 1913. After his heart attack and resulting disability in 1968 it is not surprising that he chose to return to the forest for holiday breaks at the Forest Park Hotel. It was when we, as a family joined them, that we thought to look around for a holiday cottage in the area. By a stroke of luck, Michael found the bungalow in Copse Road, Burley in 1972. He made an offer that was accepted and the rest is history.

Divorce is not an experience that I would wish on anyone. For me, it was a very traumatic experience that I found hard to deal with. My efforts over the twenty-nine years of marriage had come to nothing and I could feel my home, always so important to me, disintegrating around me. Let it be said that I did not cope very well. Inevitably, with such a break up, comes the question of money and possessions; who should have what? The divorce finally came through in 1987. Amongst the things that were awarded to me was the cottage in Burley. Over the years it had been a place of fun where we, as a family spent many a happy holiday walking in the woods, spending time on the beaches and visiting the endless supply of interesting places such as Longleat, Beaulieu, with its motor museum, Compton Acres, Portsmouth Historic Dockyard with the *Victory*, and the recovered *Mary Rose*, not to mention Paulton's Park, that became a regular haunt to celebrate birthdays. There is so much to do in this area that one would never run out of ideas. Sometimes we would venture further afield as far as Bath with its Roman Baths, Lulworth Cove, take a boat ride to the Isle of Wight to visit Queen Victoria's home, Osborne House, or to take a walk over Tennyson Down to Freshwater Bay. The cottage had become a second home, not only for us but also for many of our friends who moved in when we had no need of it. With our regular visits to the place, we had got to know many of the folk in Burley and in particular in Copse Road. They were not only acquaintances but had become good friends.

By 1990, there was no looking back. At fifty-nine, thoughts of retirement were beginning to seem like an attractive option, especially in the light of government interference in our practice of medicine. The cottage had been refashioned and partially rebuilt, with a view to retirement in mind; and my friends in Burley were increasingly saying, 'Why don't you come and live down here?' As luck would have it, our American friend, George Ray, Professor of English Literature in Lexington, Virginia, was in the UK with his students. He came down to the cottage for the weekend and we were able to talk through my situation at length and from all angles. By the time I returned to London, my decision was made; a decision which once made, always seemed to be the right one. In May 1990, the momentous move was made and I have never looked back.

The reception I received in Burley was magnificent. Neighbours and my sister-in-law, Ann, unpacked and helped to move me in. Friends in the road did everything to ensure that I settled in happily and I found that every door was open to me. All I had to do was knock and/or ask. I think of one incident that really epitomises the spirit of Burley. I had not long been here when a friend from London came to stay at a time when I had just started to do a few locums in the area. Sadly, she fell ill with pneumonia and shingles. I arrived home one evening to find her quite poorly and really not fit to be left on her own. I had a booked surgery the next day and the reason one is doing a locum is because there is no one else available. What was I to do? The next minute, the doorbell rang. Three of my neighbours, Beryl, Joan and Lucy stood there with notebook in hand. 'Tell us what needs to be done and we will do it,' they said. The next day they took over, kept her comfortable, supplied her with drinks, Lucy bed-bathed her and they made sure she was never left alone in the house. 'Thank you' was hardly enough for me to say when I arrived home, but as if that wasn't enough, the front door bell went again, five minutes later. Lucy had come with some supper for me! Where else in the world would one find such generosity?

There have been a lot of changes since our first arrival in Burley in 1973. Holiday cottages were few in number and apart from being labelled as 'grockles' we were quickly accepted and welcomed in by the people here. Everyone seemed anxious to please and encourage us, and our friends, to stay. It is a place, however, where news travels quickly. Not long after we had acquired the cottage we had a large group of friends visiting at the weekend in the midsummer. A turkey seemed to be the answer to satisfy the hunger of that number. Much to the surprise of John Moorman, the village butcher, I placed an order; he obviously was not used to people eating turkey other than in the festive season of Christmas. The day came and I went to collect the order and took it home, only to find that I did not have a suitable pan in which to cook it. Back I went to the village, to the ironmonger this time, in the hopes that he could supply a pan to fit my needs. His response was, 'I suppose that is for the turkey that you have just bought!'

Quickly one learns that one can never keep a secret in Burley, but one also learns that gossip and the spread of news is never malicious. All news travels with sympathy, empathy or joy and the response is always, 'What can I do to help?' Equally, if something needs to be done, there is always someone who can come to the rescue whether it be for plumbing, electricity, odd job or a fallen tree, everyone contributes in what they have in skills.

Since our arrival in Burley things have changed. I am no longer the only Londoner and more and more properties are being bought up by weekenders or for holiday 'lets'. Sadly, few of these people seem to join in the many village activities. Some of the ambience of the village has changed as they modernise their homes, pave their patios and safeguard their houses with high walls and imposing gateways. However, the legacy of history has not entirely been lost. Records of earlier times date back to the Bronze Age. Settlers moved in to this densely forested area and cleared small patches of land, sufficient to grow enough to supply their own needs. The fact that the land is largely infertile has ensured that acres of open farming has never been possible and so the forest remained mostly undisturbed. However, nothing ever stays the same. The Bronze Age people were followed by those of the Iron Age. Later the Romans arrived and developed a flourishing pottery industry and this was followed by further invasions by the Saxons and Vikings.

The year 1066 brought the takeover by William of Normandy. Having defeated King Harold in the battle of Hastings, William was crowned king in Westminster Abbey to mark the beginning of Norman rule. In his love of hunting and the desire to provide adequately for his table, he declared that the New Forest area was to be reserved for his personal pleasure of hunting deer and wild boar. Still today, locals object strongly to dictates from above. The local peasants and commoners of that time were no exception. They objected to the fact that they were no longer able to fence their properties, as this would 'impede the free running of the animals'. Eventually the king relented to the extent that the commoners were given grazing rights in the forest for their ponies, cattle and pigs. This right is still in operation today. Ponies and cows run wild and, in the autumn one sees pigs out for pannage, guzzling away at the fallen acorns. Acorns, if ingested by the ponies, have fatal results. The pigs serve their purpose by reducing the number of ponies lost in this way. The ponies run free in the forest and are a continual delight for the many tourists who flock here, as well as to my grandchildren as the animals stray up the road to my very gate.

More change came in the eighteenth and nineteenth centuries when some inroads were made into the forest by the felling of trees, in order to build ships. The second Lord Montague of Beaulieu sank his wealth into a fleet of ships that was to develop trade with the West Indies. In order to create a free port through which to land the goods here in England, he embarked on the building of a town on his estate, by the river, which would serve as a free port for the imports. Disastrous, from his point of view, as the ships were lost and his finances decimated. Thus, the building work was forced to stop. Hence the two rather stark rows of Georgian cottages which we see today. It so happened that at this time there was a big demand for wooden ships for the navy. This site of Buckler's Hard was ideally situated for the purpose. It was on the river and so ships would have ready access to the sea. There was a plentiful supply of wood, in particular oak trees in the forest, and Lord Montague needed the money. The ship yards were created and the ships built, some of which took part in the Battle of Trafalgar in 1805.

Even then, the usefulness of the New Forest was not lost to the nation. In World War II, the woods and houses on the Beaulieu estate were ideal for the training of spies for Special Operations. A small airfield was created nearby, from which the trained personnel could be flown and dropped into enemy, or occupied, territory. During their time in training they had the opportunity to stay in homes that were set up in French, German or other traditions, so that they could experience the sort of lives with which they might be involved on their missions. The operation remained a closely guarded secret and the fact that Odette Churchill and Violette Szabo had been through the training schools here did not become public until after the end of the war. It must have taken considerable courage to volunteer for this Service, not only courage but they were required to be fluent in the language and to understand the customs of the country into which they would be dropped. Odette Churchill, who had been born in France, did actually survive the war, having first been landed near Cannes in France in 1942. The following year she was arrested, imprisoned and tortured and condemned to death but taken to Ravensbrück concentration camp. Somehow she avoided execution and was able to testify against her guards in 1946, at the war crimes trial. Honours were then showered on her in the form of the George Cross and she was appointed a Chevalier de la Légion d'Honneur for her work with the French resistance. Violette Szabo was not so lucky. She also had been born in France and so was fluent in the language. She was parachuted behind the German lines in 1944 where she reorganised a French resistance network. On her second mission she was captured, interrogated and tortured before being also taken to Ravensbrück to be executed in 1945. She was only twenty-three years old. Her George Cross was awarded posthumously.

Tourism is now a major industry in the forest. Beaulieu attracts many of the tourists who come to view its fine National Motor Museum. Cars, coaches, bicycles, campers and hikers fill the street, shops and cafés of the villages around. Burley is no exception. Although we avoid the centre of the village when it is packed in this way, we need wander only a few yards from the main roads to find ourselves in the solitude of the forest or surrounding moors.

In spite of these invasions, there is still a nucleus of original Burleyites and others like myself, who have now been accepted. In fact I have been stripped of my title of grockle. I have even graduated from the half-grockle stage. We are a close-knit group who never seems to miss the opportunity of a get-together over a coffee morning, fund-raising activity or the annual Burley Show where gardeners compete with their fruit, vegetables and flowers, and others with their baking, photography and art work. The standard of the entries is amazing. I am particularly lucky to be living in Copse Road, a very caring road where each looks after the other. We celebrated the other day with a Copse Road party. In spite of the snow and ice, we had a trawl of over forty, nearly everyone in the road. It seemed to be a popular event with requests for another one next year.

There is so much going on in the village that one has to be careful not to take on too much. I have restricted myself to the WI, the British Legion, the Travel Club and a bit of bridge, with the proviso that I like to enjoy the game without fear of post mortems. We are lucky to have the WI hall, the Myrtle Hall, in our road, where we meet once a month for a talk followed by tea, sandwiches and cakes.

One really good thing about the WI is that they are all expert cake makers. The meetings are varied and interesting. Subjects vary from travel to flower arranging, cookery, the history of *Dad's Army*, famous places, jewellers and even the history of knickers! One has to admire those that give so much of their time to the benefit of others. Sheila runs the Over Seventies. Once a month, drivers volunteer to take the less able for a drive around the area and then back to tea in the Myrtle Hall. Annette puts in hours of research in order to organise a holiday for those who would never otherwise manage to get away. With her we have days out to places like the Hampton Court Flower show and country houses. Sometimes we enjoy breaks in England, Scotland and Ireland, and holidays abroad have included cruises on the Rhine and Dutch waterways, the States in the fall, Jersey, Slovenia and Cyprus.

There is no doubt that Burley looks after its own. When we first came to Burley, my husband was keen to join the golf club. We went to enquire, only to be greeted with long and doubtful faces. They suggested that we put our name on the waiting list but were warned that it was long, and that membership might not materialise for a very long time. My husband was disappointed and mentioned that he had hoped to play there since we had just bought the cottage in the village. Immediately, the atmosphere changed. It was a case of, 'Sign here!' 'Why don't your wife and children join as well!' We signed on the dotted line and handed over the fee of £9 for all five of us.

The caring did not stop with me. Following the death of my father in 1982, my mother had moved into a flat in Blackheath. She had settled remarkably well, was close enough to the church to be able to walk there by herself; she had thrown herself into life there, making aprons for sales of work and making new friends. Inevitably life became more difficult for her and many of her friends were less mobile and some dying. Old age is not the happiest time of life. She loved coming down to the cottage for holidays and when here, she got to know my friends, John and Wendy, who ran a rest home, Wayside, round the corner from me in Garden Road. After a couple of short stays there she decided to make the momentous decision and move down. In 1990, at the age of eighty-five, she moved down to Burley and although she always missed London, she found herself in a place where she was beautifully cared for, allowed to personalise her own room and free to walk round the village if she felt so inclined. True to form, Burley welcomed her in. She enjoyed the round of coffee mornings and jumble sales and was renowned for her success in the raffles. The Burley residents also lived up to their reputation of hospitality with invitations to friends in their homes and drives out in their cars. Several times, her sister, Dorothy, came down for holidays and great fun was had by all. I recall one evening when we had some neighbours in to meet them. My aunt, at the age of ninety, was in great form. All the old stories were related to the amusement of everyone. I only hope that I, at ninety, will be able to bid my visitors goodbye as laughter drives them to their knees and they must almost crawl out of the door.

Burley is not only a place for the elderly but also for the very young. The residents have an excellent village primary school, the Little Deers for the pre-school children, Boy Scouts, cubs and beavers groups, as well as another for the Youth of Burley (YOBS); not the yobs we hear of on the television. That apart, it is an ideal place for the young to enjoy a holiday. For me it has been a bonus and an opportunity to get to know my grandchildren. They have come in two batches: the eldest five, Joanna, Nicola, Louise, Penny and Lee are now fully fledged, and now there are another four grandchildren, Daniel, Sophie, James and Rose, together with two great-grand-children, Henry and Ruby. They are able to repeat the fun and excitement all over again. They have to play games in the 'tree house', amongst the gnarled roots of an old oak tree in the woods, take long walks in the forest and across the moors and search for fungi buried amongst the fallen leaves of autumn. Summer days take them to the beaches along the coast. They love to get together and love to get together here. Hopefully, their friendships will last a lifetime.

Some memories particularly stand out in my mind. A favourite of mine was the evening when I was in charge. They were all bathed, shining and ready for bed – or so I had hoped. They were not quite so sure that it was really bedtime. For some time I heard much chatter and many giggles from upstairs until I decided that it was time to go and read the riot act to them. They just forestalled me. There they stood, looking guilty but angelic, bearing a large sheet of paper on which was a pile of feathers and two paper eyes. With it was a note that read, 'We've made this for you Grandma, because we love you

16. Michael, my husband and me 1952

17. Home Guard duty 1941 – my Grandpa Watkins

18. Cups for British Junior and West of England championships 1951

19. My graduation day 1955

20. Lakeside Health Centre – Thamesmead 1970s

21. Goodbye Thamesmead – Rodney Turner and Peter Higgins – partners/Lakeside and me 1990

22. *The family 1995*

23. *Family gathering 2004*

24. At award as Serving Sister of the Order of St Johns with Joan Gilbert 1989

25. Occasion of FRCGP award – with President and my family – 2004

26. Travelling companions L–R – Maggie, Norma, Margaret, Betty, George, Rhoda and Jules and me

27. James and Lee McMillan 2009 – Andrew's children, grandchildren

28. James and Rose McMillan – grandchildren – 2009 – Andrew's children

29. Daniel and Sophie Williams – grandchildren – 2009 – Carol's children

30. *Jan and Greg and the girls – grandchildren – Nicola, Louise and Penny 1996*

31. *The Griffiths family – Joanna: granddaughter, Henry and Ruby: great-grandchildren and Andy 2007*

so much – it is an owl'. The owl is now framed and hangs on my wall as one of my most treasured possessions. As for the eiderdown from which the feathers came, it is no more. A small price to pay for such a gift, and the eiderdown was very old and leaking anyway.

The other really big bonus for me was the frequent visits from my grandson, Lee. From about the age of five until he left school, he regularly came down to Burley for his school holidays. Here he could relax, have fun, get to know the neighbours and make new friends. Some of his time was spent at the Avon Tyrell Centre not far from here. They run sessions for children in the holiday period. Under supervision they built shelters, climbed trees, searched for wildlife and played football and here he made one particular friend, Danny. Still when Lee comes down for a visit we have to visit all the old haunts, his old golf coach Chris Brooks and catch up, once again with Danny. Even though they are now grown, working men, I am not excluded. Each evening after supper, I am summoned to the table to play racing demon. Perhaps it is my age but I no longer win!

Now they have discovered the excitements of Halloween and I have a regular booking with those that want, once again, to dress as witches, wizards, bats and owls so that they can join in the fun and parade through the street. Halloween is celebrated in style in a village that boasts connections with witches. Some say that this dates from the time when smuggling was rife in the area, during the eighteenth and nineteenth centuries. Smugglers making their way from the coast, along the forest tracks, must keep a watchful eye out for the soldiers trying to intercept them. Consequently, there was much whispering in the bushes, as well as the woman, Lovey Warne, with a red petticoat, who used to stand at what is now known as Warnes Lane. If the patrol was out she would display her red petticoat as a silent warning sign; hence the name of the road. Burley must have been a big centre for this trade. Our seventeenth century village pub, the Queen's Head underwent major reconstruction work during which a cellar was found. In it were stashed pistols, coins and alcohol that must have been left by the smugglers.

The witch myth, until as recently as the 1960s, was perpetuated by a woman by the name of Sybil Leek She claimed to be a white witch, was said to practise positive magic, and she would wander through the village with her pet jackdaw. Having lived with gypsies for years, she was known to be an authority on New Forest life. Now, the myth adds to the list of tourist attractions in Burley, as witchlike goods are sold in the Witches Coven and other like-minded shops. It seems that one can learn the art of writing, preparing and casting one's own spells either by studying books or joining a coven. Maybe this is one of the arts that I shall not pursue myself.

Another regular attraction is the annual village pantomime. We boast a group, resurrected in 1987, known as the Burley Players. For hours they gather and rehearse for the show that takes us all back to childhood. We in the audience repeatedly take our cues of boos for the villain, cheers for the goodie, the 'Oh yes it is' and 'Oh no it isn't', not to mention the old faithful, 'It's behind you'. The performers reach almost professional standards and regularly achieve the mention of Best Panto in the Forest. It, too, is one of the events that draws the village together. School children take to the stage, the artists organise the scenery, dressmakers the costumes, stage hands set the scenes and those that understand these things, manipulate the lights. It is a concerted effort.

One major event that seemed to draw all the villagers together was that of the Millenium celebrations. For a whole weekend in the year 2000, we enjoyed special church services, displays of the talents of the patchwork group and artists of Burley, a tea party in the grounds of the manse, fancy dress parade and displays on the village green by each of the various groups in the village. Many also opened their gardens for public viewing. I did them all and very beautiful they were too.

CHAPTER 14

A second career (1990 to present timc)

WHEN I RETIRED FROM Thamesmead in 1990, I thought that was it. I was fifty-nine and moving to a new area, an area in which I had never before been involved in medicine. I have always loved my job, in fact there have been times when, at my lowest ebb, it has been my lifeline. This sudden exodus from the profession was going to leave an enormous gap. How would I now fill my time? I need not have worried. Somehow, things fell into place and I have had to resign myself to the fact that I am the sort of person who will always have too much to do, and to be honest, that is the way I like it.

After a few weeks in the New Forest, it became obvious that if I wanted to continue leading a full life, I would have to earn the necessary to be able to achieve it. Initially, I did not feel that I wanted to be tied to any one practice and so, put my name on the list of 'Locums available'. Quickly, it seemed that there was no shortage of locum opportunities and this gave me the chance to work in a number of different practices and family planning clinics, to get to know the people involved and to consider which of these practices I felt I could perhaps get involved with long term. It was also an opportunity to observe first-hand how the medical profession was adapting to the dictates that followed the ruling of the *Health of the Nation* Green Paper of 1991. When I discussed this with the doctors with whom I was now working, I was reassured that I had made absolutely the right choice to retire at that stage. Their struggle to keep up with the continually changing goal posts, often introduced without the benefit of a prior pilot study, found them of necessity, obeying the rules, but with a changed attitude. No longer were they the dedicated workers who enjoyed their job, but had decided that their only choice was to work mainly for the money and hope to retire as soon as possible.

After about a year I had settled into life in Burley, made plenty of friends and had a constant stream of visitors who liked to enjoy a break in the country. I still needed to work, especially if I wanted to continue with my travelling exploits. Also, although locum work had been good in many ways, I missed continuity in dealing with patients and I missed belonging to a unit. In fact, there were occasions when I felt just part of the furniture. When I thought about what I might want to do, I decided that in an ideal world, I would like a part-time job in general practice for two or three days a week, with no night or weekend work and little or no involvement on the administrative side. I also thought it would be nice to get a regular session in the family planning clinic once a week. I had already taken on a small amount of counselling work at home and to my amazement, I was offered three posts on my terms. I had been working fairly regularly in the practice at the Winton Health Centre in Bournemouth. The senior partner, with a young family, decided that she would like to mark down her hours and so I was offered a job share position at the Centre, in which I continued for the next five years before retiring once again. I seem to have retired so often that it is hard to know how many times I have said goodbye. Once again, this retirement was not final and I continued to do locums and medical examinations for the practice for a good many more years.

On the family planning front, I was also able to be enlisted on to the staff of the East Dorset Health Authority. I joined it at a time when a keen, enthusiastic team that kept abreast of modern developments was working together to provide a first-class service. By 1994 it was decided to open a Youth Advisory Service in the Bournemouth area and I was appointed as one of the medical officers at the newly opened premises named The Junction. It was a new venture catering for the many youngsters needing help and advice. The idea was to 'promote positive sexual health and enable young people to experience healthy sexual development and maturation'. The centre was already funded by the Children's Society, where advice regarding housing benefits, jobs, legal matters and emotional support was available. Young people were already used to coming to the centre, thus the threat of attending a strange place with unknown personnel was not a problem. Initially we held two sessions a week at which a doctor was present. A nurse, trained in family planning, was on the premises between 3.30 p.m. and 6 p.m. every weekday and Saturday morning. She, as the nurse who also attended the schools for sessions on education in sexual health, was already known and accepted by the youngsters who referred to her as Auntie Pat.

The youngsters attended the clinic largely for advice regarding contraception, but so often other problems were revealed for which we could offer support, advice or counselling as well as the necessary attention if problems of sexually transmitted diseases were found. Superficially one might consider the very young to be irresponsible and foolish in their behaviour, but so often one found an unhappy child seeking love and caring, where this might have been lacking in the home. They might suffer the scars of parental break up, new partners moving in and the feeling that they were no longer wanted or needed at home. Others may have suffered neglect, physical or sexual abuse about which they had never previously been able to disclose. Here at The Junction, support and counselling were available along with the chance to recognise the importance of a secure relationship, not only for themselves but for their children if they came along. Coupled with this, I feel, is the problem of media hype. Increasingly, it seems that on TV all couples are prepared to pop into bed at the slightest whim and after the briefest of acquaintance. Certainly, in my years working at The Junction, things changed. Initially it would be a young girl or boy, in a steady relationship, wanting to ensure that a pregnancy did not occur. So often nowadays, it is a question of a night out for a bit of fun, which involves 'getting drunk and having sex'. One does really wonder how they will settle to a stable relationship and provide a secure background for their children in later life.

There is much talk nowadays about the dangers of sex education, encouraging loose and promiscuous behaviour. It may be that the best instruction should come from within the home but not every parent finds this an easy task. In my school days, admittedly a long time ago, the school considered itself to be extremely 'modern'. Every parent had to give consent for us to attend a special sex education lesson. I well recall our biology teacher, a confirmed spinster, dressed in twin set, ankle socks and sandals, drawing a picture of a frog on the blackboard, before continuing to relate the facts of life to us. Maybe we were rather green, but it seemed, on our release, that few had understood what she was on about. We had to rely on our more knowledgeable friends to fill us in. As for leaving it to the family, my mother, who never talked about that sort of thing, thought she was being very 'with it' when she took me to one side on the eve of my marriage, at a time when I had already qualified in medicine and had held an obstetric post. She continued, 'I think, my dear, there is something that I should tell you . . .' We have come a long way since those days and the instruction now given at schools should help to fill the gap, but I would hope that the discussions are not just about the mechanics of unions but also thoughts about the importance of relationships and also how to say 'No' when it is not the right time.

Things have changed a lot in the wider field of family planning as a whole. It was not until 1921 that the first birth control clinic was opened in London by Marie Stopes. In the following ten years a further five birth control societies opened up clinics throughout England with the slogan, 'Children by choice, not chance'. However, to start with, the service was only for married women in whom a further pregnancy would be detrimental to health and it was not until 1952 that the clinics would give contraceptive advice also, to women who were about to be married. By the end of the fifties I undertook the training in family planning, at a time when the barrier methods were all that were on offer. It was not until 1961 that the contraceptive pill became available in the clinics, which eventually allowed women to take proper control of their lives, as well as take the more controversial step of being freer with their sexual favours. Change came too with the passing of the Abortion Act in 1967, allowing abortion up to the twenty-fourth week of pregnancy in situations where there is substantial risk to the woman's life or physical or mental health of herself or her children or at any stage if there are foetal abnormalities. This has led to a greater choice for women with an unwanted pregnancy and spared the sometimes disastrous results of illegal abortion.

Things have also changed dramatically in the last few years in the management of the clinics. With the constant pressures on funding and the need for 'cut backs' to save money, staffing and clinics have been reduced and pressure on the remaining workers seriously increased, with resulting stress, overwork, dissatisfaction and poor morale, so much so, that many have handed in their notice. Our enthusiastic, dedicated team has been lost and patient satisfaction reduced. As for saving money, this aim is not always achieved. Extra expense may ensue as unwanted pregnancies end in termination and sexually transmitted diseases, including AIDS are on the increase. It always seems that demands for savings come from on high, distanced from the people on the ground who really understand what the job is all about. Constant audits, targets, validation, not to mention Health and Safety, and attempts to avert the problems of litigation add greatly to the cost. One wonders if they really do achieve anything for the patient.

Following my visit to China in 1978, I had kept a camera in the cupboard in my surgery so that I might take pictures of interesting conditions as they came through the door. As I had anticipated, these pictures were invaluable not only for teaching both medical students and Trainees (now Registrars), but I had also learned so much and it had re-awoken my interest in medicine. What is more, the patients seemed to like it too. Whilst I might be photographing one problem, they would frequently reveal other hidden problems for me to take. Sometimes they would request a copy to show their friends, keep as a memento or take to Court to back some claim they might be making. We were fortunate at Thamesmead in that we had a number of visiting consultants from the hospital who used to come regularly to the Centre to see patients. We would sit in on these sessions so that we might discuss particular problems and learn for the future. Our pictures on these occasions were an added bonus. We could discuss them over lunch, or they might supplement a consultation of a patient in whom their rash had faded or was changing in appearance. It was particularly useful in the dermatology, gynaecological and eye sessions. I had already begun to find a place for some of the pictures in the medical journals. I could not believe the demand for such work. However, I did have some concern about my lack of knowledge in some areas. When I was a medical student, there was a distinct lack of experience in some subjects, particularly dermatology. I recall six out-patient clinics only on the subject. Seated at the back of the surgery, without the opportunity of a closer look did not exactly equip us with a full understanding of diseases of the skin or, for that matter, with a similar approach in ophthalmology. These sessions at Thamesmead did much to fill the gaps and I also had the luxury of the backing of experts to vet any article I produced.

Over the years at Thamesmead, I had already built up a large collection of pictures. From a very early stage, I had also obtained written consent from patients to use these pictures for teaching and medical literature, not only for those in which they were obviously recognisable, as where the face or tattoos were depicted, but for everything, even a spot on the leg. This has turned out to be an invaluable step. Working down in Bournemouth for all those extra years has allowed me to further increase my library. One big advantage has been that I have been able to photograph many of the very ordinary conditions; the sort that occur in general practice, but with which most people do not bother and, certainly hospital libraries do not contain. However, the occurrence of the rarer conditions in general practice is less common.

When I retired from the Winton job share, I was concerned that I would no longer be able to feed my library with new pictures or keep up to date with developments in medicine. Chance and luck were once again on my side. One of the consultants in the Dermatology Unit of the hospital allowed me to sit in with him on a session. At the end, he commented that it would be nice if I came back on a regular basis and not only that, I was appointed as a Senior House Officer in the department. I have forever to be grateful for this opportunity to learn and extend my library and add some of the more unusual dermatological problems to my library as well.

In semi-retirement I have had more time to concentrate on feeding a number of medical and nursing journals with articles based around my pictures, as well as taking on a position on the board of the journal *Practice Nursing*. They say that every picture tells a story and in this type of work, it certainly seems to be the case. It is very satisfying to see my work in print. It has been good for me, in that I have been able to keep in touch with the medical world and have contact with and meet other interesting people as well as seeing the pictures put to good use.

Exposure in this way has also led to requests for other contributions. The management of psychosocial problems has always been a great interest of mine. Through this avenue I was able to do a series of articles on the subject for a couple of journals, and was then asked to contribute to sections of a series of books being produced at Bath University on the subjects of emotional problems in women and another on emotional problems in men. The series as a whole, was said by the Royal College of General Practitioners (RCGP) 'to meet with the requirements of personal development plans and Post Graduate Educational Hours'. Having for many years been a member of the RCGP, I was also honoured by being promoted to the position of a Fellow of the College. I received my certificate, along with many others, at a grand presentation at the Bath Hotel in Bournemouth, at a ceremony at which all my family were able to attend. A rather special day, the pleasure of which was added to by the fact that one of my ex-trainees, Jon, by that time a GP in Lincolnshire, also gained the same recognition.

My interest in photography has not been limited to medicine. Since my initial China experience, the discovery of the joys of travel and the opportunity to travel widely in the world, the camera has been my constant companion. The resulting pictures are a way of retaining the many memories that I have of the trips. It is so easy to finish a two- or three-week holiday, having enjoyed a wonderful time but the details of it having merged into a blur. In order not to lose the memories, I return home with literally hundreds of pictures to be labelled and sorted, and a very full diary of the events that took place and the people we met. It is then that the hard work starts. The diary must be abridged and converted into some meaningful story. It must also be typed out in legible form before the post-holiday excitement and memories have faded. In the ordinary way my handwriting is enough of a problem for others as well as myself, to decipher. The records I make in my holiday diary as we go along, are virtually impossible to read. It has now become a habit of mine on my arrival home, to write up the trip in a shortened form, sometimes as an entry on the tour company's newsletter and/or for the other members of the group who seem now to wait for me to do the job, saying it saves them a lot of trouble! With this behind me I am able to make up a slide show to illustrate the tour and it seems that the talks that come out of these labours are popular. I applied to go on the Speakers List for the Women's Institute (WI) in Hampshire. With my name now on the WI book, I get a number of requests to do talks in the area and one talk seems to lead to another. There is always someone who knows of another group that is looking for speakers. I seem to pay regular visits, not only to the many WIs, but also the Townswomen's Guild, church groups, travel clubs, photographic groups, Age Concern, The National Trust and a group that delights in the name of CAMEO – standing for 'Come And Meet Everyone'. They seem to enjoy it and so do I. I find that it is another way of reliving my holiday. The remuneration from this is not wasted either. I tend to seek out worthy projects in the countries that we visit, the current one being a small school in a squatter settlement in Namibia, where the children would have no other opportunity of education. The education is not narrowed to the three Rs. Yes, that does come into it but they also learn how to fit into society, how to handle money, how to wash, use the loos, health care and a recent blitz on AIDS in which the adults in the settlement have been involved as well. In fact, free condoms are available at the door; so necessary in a country with a frighteningly high rate of the disease, where 30 per cent of the population are said to be HIV positive.

No, so-called retirement is never dull and should there be a few spare moments, in a village such as ours, there are always some less fortunate than myself. Hours living alone, unable to get out without assistance, can seem to be forever, unless a head pops round the door. For the visitor, this is not a chore. These people have a wealth of past that is fascinating, if one just has a few moments to listen and learn from it. It doesn't stop at conversation, outings or shopping, I have also learned from experts how to play Scrabble.

CHAPTER 15

Unforgettable days

WHEN ONE LOOKS BACK ON one's life there are certain days and occasions that stand out in memory above all the others. Memories of my early childhood tend to be more fleeting and patchy, but those in later life often remain as clear to me as if it were yesterday. For some reason it is still the most worrying, darkest or frightening that remain uppermost but amongst them are days of fun, hilarity and joy.

There may be days, such as when we went to Kew Gardens in London. With my friend Doreen, we took both of our young families and a couple of other children, ten of us in all. It was a beautiful day, the sky was blue, the sun was shining and the children were excited. Kew Gardens was always a special place for me and particularly appealing to a large crowd such as ours, when in the 1970s, the entrance fee was only 3d. (three old pence) per person. As soon as we entered the gate the children were off on their exploration of the gardens, hot houses and intriguing pathways. By the end of the day they had done it all, including enjoying a picnic by the lake. In the midday sun, the temperature rose and the children were feeling the heat. However, they soon discovered ways of counteracting this when they discovered the many hosepipes spraying water on the lawns and plants all round the garden. Cooling under the spray and falling in the lake were just the remedies they wished for. I still recall my friend and I leaving the gardens, bearing a pile of wet clothes and with the children stripped down to their underpants, while we tried to pretend that they did not belong to us. A great day had been had by all.

Yes, some family days are particularly special, sometimes because of the event, sometimes because some things become traditional and were part of the life of my own childhood but carried down to the next generations. For us, the game of racing demon is a must when we holiday together. When the day is done and bedtime in the offing, what better than to sit around the table for this rather noisy, vicious game? For those who have not managed to learn the intricacies of this adaptation of the calmer demon patience that can be played when alone, each of us, sometimes up to as many as ten, is given a pack of playing cards. A starter shouts, 'Ready, Steady, Go' and we are off. Speed is of the essence as we try to build up cards at the centre of the table from the ace up to the king. Each suit has a separate pile, with every person round the table trying to add their own cards first, thereby causing problems, if two are attempting to add to a pile at the same time. The excitement is intense, but vicious though the game may sound, it is played with good humour and without tears.

There was one year when we were all on holiday in France. My granddaughter, Penny, was only five years old and had not reached the age when she could cope with racing demon. Our second choice of game, Up Jenkins, seemed to be the obvious alternative. Our two teams lined up, one on each side of the table. The game involves the hiding of a small coin in a hand of one member of one of the teams. At the words, 'Up Jenkins' – everyone in the team must raise their hands above the table before being instructed, by the others, to form a 'bridge', 'spider', perform a 'creepy crawly' or just bang their hands flat on the table at the words, 'smash 'em'. The other team must then guess who has the coin. We all felt a bit sorry for our youngest member, Penny, and wondered if she would be able to cope. We need not have worried; it was she, continually bearing a look of innocence, who managed to deceive us every time. She won our hearts, as well as the game.

Birthdays were always celebrated with a party. School friends were invited, tea was enjoyed and games appropriate to the age group were organised. When it came to my son, Andrew's eighth birthday, I felt that I would not be able to cope with twenty-five over-excited boys, and so enlisted the services of a magician. We gathered round him after tea and they watched intently, trying to catch him out or learn how to do the trick themselves. It was when he started on the trick of 'hiding the toffee' that our dog Mahler, began to get interested. She moved to the front row and followed the path of the toffee from his hand to his hat, behind his ear and then . . .? The look of disappointment on the dog's face was obvious, as the hoped for prize was lost. Our magician had fooled not only the children but also our four-legged friend.

There are days when the best made plans do not live up to expectations. There was one day when we had a houseful at the cottage in Burley. Michael and I were down with the three children, our good friend Jenny and Ann, my sister-in-law, was over with her three children, Margaret, Richard and David. The weather was not on our side, the clouds looked ominous and rain was threatening. The question of what to do was uppermost in our thoughts. Michael had decided that he would like to be the one to plan the day, so we waited, with impatience, for some decision to be made, but by lunch-time none had been forthcoming. Unable to bear it any longer I made the suggestion that we might visit the Shell House in Southbourne. I had heard on television that it was worth a visit. However, as we arrived at said house, we realised that we had made a big mistake. The weather did not help. It was pouring with rain and the house had to be viewed from the outside. It appeared that the owner had travelled the world, brought back shells from every corner of the globe, and stuck them on the outside of his house and in the garden. Michael took one look and decided not to get out of the car. The rest of us, having made the effort, went to have a closer look only to find that, apart from the shell-covered house, there were plaques mounted amongst the shells, of pious quotations placed all around the garden – and in the grotto. By this time the children had lost all interest while Jenny, Ann and myself were doing our best to put a brave face on it. As we viewed the latest ditty in the grotto and feeling that it was almost the last straw, two women came up behind us. Their conversation went like this: 'What a marvelous man he must be to have done all this. It is truly wonderful'. We three said nothing, there was no need. We all shared the same sense of humour. A quick exchange of glances was followed by hysterical laughter that continued until we got back to the car. I am not sure whether Michael was upset that he might have missed out on something or whether he just thought that we were mad.

Together we had a lot of fun, even when involved in the serious game of golf. There was one day when I set off with the children with Michael following behind on the next hole with the 'good' golfers. We had reached the seventh hole. My ball was placed some twenty yards from the hole but behind a tree. I would not pretend to be a good golfer. Even to hit the ball squarely was, for me, quite an achievement. On this occasion, I took my club and made perfect contact. The ball headed straight in the direction of the hole but, sadly, the tree was in the way. The ball hit the tree and bounced back at my feet – not once, not twice but three times. Three perfect shots without an inch of progress. There were some disapproving looks from the serious foursome on the hole behind us as we fell to our knees with laughter. The occasion is still not forgotten and regularly comes up when we meet.

As a teenager, I vividly remember my first visit to Wimbledon. I always enjoyed the game of tennis and the chance to go and watch the best was exciting enough, but what I had not anticipated was the thrill of hearing the cheers or groans radiating from the tiers of the ivy-covered Centre Court, as a point was won or lost. On this first visit we had arrived late in the afternoon when play was in full swing. For the next few years, the Wimbledon fortnight was a must for me. Regularly we queued all night to gain entry to the standing area on the Centre Court. The queuing was all part of the fun as we ate our sandwiches, were entertained by the buskers and kipped down for the night. It was mainly the men's singles that attracted our attention and we have memories of the struggles of the heroes of the day. My first year at a final was in 1946 when a Frenchman, Yvon Petra, won the title. Later this was followed by Falkenburg (1948), who seemed to spend much time lying on the ground, Frank Sedgeman, Jaroslav Drobny, and the great Australian couple, Hoad and Rosewall. The achievement of my medical degree in 1955 put an end to all this but still, Wimbledon is an important fixture on my calendar. Watching it on the box does not create quite the same atmosphere but it is a good second.

Maybe, there is something about queuing that adds to the experience of some major event. Even in my younger days, the thought of standing in a queue for six or eight hours at night did not seem appealing. However, on the one occasion we did, the unique atmosphere around us added immensely to the event. It was the night that we decided to go to the lying in state of Winston Churchill. It is not a journey that I would have made for many, but for me who had lived through the war years, he was my hero. His grasp of oratory was unmatched and when in the war we had listened to his bold, confident speeches, the perfectly chosen words rang in our ears and we felt inspired. We knew that we would, 'Never give in'. In that queue over Westminster Bridge, as far as our entry to the Westminster Hall where he lay, those years and the same spirit of the people were revived. It was not a sad queue, it was one of gratitude and celebration of the man that we felt had saved us. Reverence came to the fore as soon as we entered the Hall, as one of the 321,360 others who had come to pay homage, and quietly filed past his coffin.

Other particularly moving moments have occurred on my travels; moments such as that bleak December day, when we stood at the top of the Great Wall of China in 1978. It was in the days before tourism and we had it to ourselves, amongst the grandeur of the surrounding rugged country and steep mountains, with the wall snaking its way into the distance. We were cold and it was snowing but any discomforts melted away as we viewed this part of the 4,000 mile wall that was built by China's first Emperor, Qui Shi Huang of the third century BC, to protect the northern borders of his empire from the Mongolians and other invaders. It is sad to think of the numbers, probably over a million, who died in the construction of this great project but amazing to think that after 2,000 years, it still stands for all to see. One has to pinch oneself to check that one is really there.

Sometimes, one is hit by unexpected moments of magic. We were in the south of Argentina, near the small town of Calafate, not far from the Chilean border. We had come to see the Moreno glacier in this isolated spot. For eternity, this glacier has been slowly making its way for some nineteen miles from the heights of the Patagonian ice-fields in Chilean mountains, to the waters of the Lake Argentina, by which we stood. These ice-fields rate in importance for their reserve of fresh water. They are said to hold the third largest reserve in the world. We were deposited at this spectacle in the National Park of the Glaciers by our guide, who then announced that she would be returning for us in two and a half hours' time. Fortunately the weather was fine and sunny and the wind not too chill, but nevertheless we wondered what on earth we would do with ourselves in this bleak place for that length of time. All I can say to anyone left in this situation, two and a half hours is not long enough to absorb the wonders of this place. From the pure white crags of ice there emanates an intense cobalt blue colour, enhancing its beauty. Surprising too, is the fact that this apparently solid block of ice is not static, it is constantly on the move as it slowly advances at the rate of about a metre a day. Its progress is alive with sound: cracks like pistol shots as the ice splits, rumbles and thunderous roars as chunks fall off at the face to drift on to the lake as icebergs, and the sound of great gushes of water as they are released from under the ice. It is hard to comprehend the size of this great glacier, one of the few Patagonian glaciers that is not retreating. At its face it is about three miles wide, stands about 240 feet above the water line and in total has a depth of 558 feet. We were mesmerised by our magic moments and felt privileged to be there.

Never does everything in life go according to plan. It is also said that 'troubles never come singly'. Certainly both these statements were true on one fateful midsummer's day in 1965, which was undoubtedly the worst day of my life. It was Saturday and my weekend on call for the practice. The phone went early in the morning to say that my grandfather was ill. I called my boss, who very nobly volunteered to take over until I had sorted things out. By the time I arrived at my grandfather's home, the doctor had been and diagnosed a strangulated hernia; my grandfather was to be taken to Farnborough Hospital where he was admitted. By mid-morning I had to leave him as he was about to go down to the theatre for surgery. I was warned that at his age, then ninety-one, he might not pull through. I arrived home to find that Janet had bad stomach ache. Michael had called the doctor and it was suspected that she had an appendicitis. We took her down to the hospital, Lewisham this time, where I waited until Jan had successfully undergone her operation, was back on the ward and doing OK. There was then just time to return to Farnborough to find that my grandfather had returned from the theatre, having survived the surgery. Exhausted, but thankful, I returned home in the early evening. On informing my boss that the invalids were all right, her response was to hand work back to me so that I could take any further calls that night. They say that there is no peace for the wicked. I was called out three times.

One of the things that seemed to be omitted from my medical training was how to deal with difficult or dangerous patients. I understand that today one must attend a course on the subject and collect the right bit of paper to say that one is competent to deal with such a situation. I suppose it is a step in the right direction but it cannot possibly cover all eventualities. Maybe it is just as important to follow one's instinctive reactions at the time, when faced with a problem. I have survived, and learned each time, but then the next time is always different. I recall in my very early days as a locum in a strange hospital, being called urgently to the ward. A large, powerful man had been admitted following a head injury and had become aggressive, indeed violent. By the time I arrived, he was struggling to free himself from the six or seven staff who were holding him down. What on earth, as a young junior houseman, was I to do? In fact the problem resolved itself as they released their grip and he turned to me. Free from the restraint, he relaxed as we talked through his situation.

My next encounter was not long after starting in general practice. I received a call to say that one of our patients had gone berserk and was smashing up his home. I knew the man and liked him. He had always presented as a meek and mild character who worked as a road sweeper. This is surely not the most exciting job, but one could admire someone who was prepared to sweep his way through life rather than sponge off the state. Sadly his wife had recently died and he found himself distressed and unable to cope. I realised that something would have to be done but did not fancy facing it alone. First I telephoned our local psychiatric consultant and asked him to do a domiciliary visit with me. 'Oh,' he said, 'you don't want to worry about that, just go and give him an injection and that should calm him down'. Bravery is not my strong point. I felt strongly that I did need support in my mission. First I rang the social worker and the police asking them to meet me outside his home at 5 p.m. I arrived at the house at 5 o'clock. The social worker never appeared and the police said, 'If he sees our uniforms, it might upset him; it is better that you go in yourself while we wait round the corner'.

Tentatively I rang the bell. Mr S let me in. The scene that met me was unbelievable. Everything was smashed, broken glass everywhere and furniture strewn at all angles. I sat down on the one remaining upright chair and suggested that I could help him by giving him an injection. He did not seem to like the idea. He stood in front of me, put his hand in his pocket and pointed something at me. 'Don't move,' he said, 'I've got a gun in here'. As I sat there, with my previous life surging though my brain, I knew not what to do. After what seemed like a very long time he put his hand in the other pocket and pulled out a whistle, saying, 'I'm going to call the police'. Sure enough, he did just that. He went to the door and blew the whistle and the police came running. I do not know if he ever understood why they took him away and not me!

CHAPTER 16

Looking back

FOR ME, THE WRITING OF THIS autobiography has been an incredibly interesting exercise. One goes through life, lives through a variety of experiences but rarely stops to take breath and understand the effect that all this has had on oneself as a person. I have been surprised how, putting pen to paper, has actually taken me back to past days, good and bad. With an adult mind I have once again been the child, the teenager, the adult, the parent, the doctor as well as, today, one classed amongst the elderly. It has made me think. Am I the person I am today because of my inherited genes or have the experiences that I have lived through been the bigger influence on my life? Coming from a family of seafarers and adventurers, is my love of travel 'in the blood', the result of the stories brought back by my grandfather after his momentous trip around the world, or just the fact that I have been so lucky to have had the opportunity, and finances, to be able to make these journeys?

There is no doubt that luck and opportunity, are a big factor. Luck has been on my side in many areas. Firstly, I chose the right parents, or at least the right parents for me. I was in a family that cared and wanted the best for me. The family unit was very important and it was due to good fortune that my father was in a reserved occupation and not called up to fight in World War II. None of our family died in the war. Officially our family was not separated in the war years, but, even so, those years have left their mark on me. I feel that the sudden changes that occurred during this time must have something to do with the fact that I still resist change at every turn, even though when changes have come, they always seem to have been for the good. Nevertheless the underlying fear of change still persists. Those unhappy years when I was left behind at boarding school in Seascale, have no doubt, contributed to my horror of institutional life. Those bad times were also associated with failure when I could not keep up with school work. It was so much better, indeed exciting, when I returned to London and started to succeed, both in class and in sport.

I presume this has contributed to my competitive nature in that I need to do well and receive approval, sometimes to the detriment of those around me. The game of squash fitted perfectly into the scheme of things and, as luck would have it, the squash club was just across the road from our home at a time when Ruth set up her teaching programme for beginners. It was easily accessible for a quick game at any time of the day, after dark or in inclement weather. This simple combination of factors led to many years of involvement in this all-absorbing and exciting sport.

I should forever be grateful to my father who encouraged me to go into medicine. I had entered the profession with some doubts about coping with the responsibility involved, however, with my youthful enthusiasm; I felt that maybe that was an art that could be learned. Looking back, I cannot think of any job that would have suited me better. Even in this area, luck has played a very major part. Very early on, having embarked on married life I realised that my rather high-flying notions of becoming a surgeon, requiring years of 'living in' at the hospital, would be impossible. Child health clinics crossed my mind, but when fairly early in my life, it became clear that I must earn my 'keep', the offer of a Trainee in a general practice post down the road seemed the obvious choice. Circumstances dictated my decision. Here I was involved with people in a practice based on practising good medicine and accepting new ideas. After my initiation here, no other branch of medicine would have been right for me. People have always interested me much more than the diseases from which they suffer.

The visit to China in 1978 that revolutionised my life was, yet again, a mere stroke of chance. It has reshaped my later years, kept me employed and more than busy. Fortunately, it seems that I have been able to take these chances, grab them with both hands and allow them to enrich my life. Now, I am reaping the rewards of a more than fulfilled retirement.

For me, my marriage break-up was a disaster. It had never been a good marriage but it was one on which I had never wanted to give up. I had struggled to 'make things work', acted the part of 'happy families' and always hoped that things would right themselves. When it came to the crunch I was devastated, exhausted and unable to cope. It is in such times of trouble that one finds one's friends. They, and the children, rallied round, supported me and gave me reason to go on living. I was so lucky that they were there. Now, I look back at the life I lead today and realise that, if Michael were still around, so much of the good that I now enjoy would never have been possible.

Luck was on my side yet again, with the arrival of my children. Inevitably in the course of rearing children there are both moments of joy and also of worry and concern. It is hard to let go when they reach the notorious teenage years; however, we weathered the storms and have come out the other side. They now welcome me into their homes or visit me, with their children, down in the New Forest, to repeat some of the fun that we enjoyed in days gone by. What more could one ask?

Luck is not only important in relation to one's immediate circumstances, but also enormously affected by the times in which one lives. For me, it was normal to be able to study medicine, plan my family and go to the ballot box on election day, but to be born at any time in the previous sixty years, life would have been very different. In a matter of only one generation, women have been liberated in so many ways. It was as late as 1870 that the struggles of Elizabeth Garrett Anderson gained her the eventual award of an MD degree in medicine and the ability to practise. Had it not been for her, the opportunities for people like myself, might never have been possible. Maybe I was born too early to receive the so-called benefits of the EU directives. My working hours were not restricted, I did not receive overtime if I worked longer hours, there was no provision for maternity leave with pay, nor the protection of a job to be waiting for me on my return a year later. In our day we had to hand in our notice and find another job if or when we were ready. What is more, interviewers were allowed to ask what arrangements we would have in place for child care; of course one's employers need to know that you will not be taking time off every time someone is ill at home. However, it was not all bad and at least I did receive the same salary as the men, small though it was and managed, in a short time, to gain a wealth of experience. Since those days, I have also been fortunate to always be able to work part-time. In a full-time post, I feel I could never have coped and certainly could never have continued so long in medicine.

Medicine, itself, has changed so much in the fifty years with which I have been involved. When I qualified we had the benefit of the earlier antibiotics, steroids were just beginning to be available and new drugs were beginning to evolve. The thought of transplant surgery was never even dreamt of until Dr Christian Barnard performed the first heart transplant in 1967, at the Groote Schuur Hospital in Cape Town, South Africa. Now it seems that almost every organ is transplantable, as well as thoughts about gene therapy that foresees the possibility of treating inherited diseases which are caused by defective genes, and might include problems such as manic depression, Alzheimer's, heart disease and diabetes. The possible list seems to grow all the time, and only time will show if these possibilities mature into reality.

Close on its heels are thoughts about cloning. Dolly the sheep was created as long ago as 1996. She survived for seven years and died with a form of lung cancer common to sheep. There has been much discussion as to the ethics of such a procedure, but currently there are hopes that it could be used to preserve the continuation of some endangered species and to mount a programme for the recreation of 'spare parts' for humans. One would hope that this would reduce the risk of rejection following transplant surgery, and overcome the shortage of donors in this field. So far, the success rate in cloning is poor with more than 90 per cent of cloning attempts failing to result in viable offspring but in the meantime, discussions continue on the advisability of allowing human cloning. Legislation to ban it is being considered but I personally would have considerable fears about the production of 'made to measure man'. Perhaps I am fortunate in that I should never have to find out what that might mean.

Women's place in society used to be different, too. It was only in 1918, just thirteen years before my birth that some women were given the right to vote, providing they were over thirty and occupied premises of a yearly value of not less that £5 (a lot of money in those days). Equality with the men did not follow until 1928, when women gained equal rights with the men, and their voting age was reduced to twenty-one, in line with the men at that time. Their rights had not easily been achieved. Emily Pankhurst and her family, as suffragettes, were to the fore in a variety of protests, and suffered a number of stints in prison for their trouble, while one, Emily Davison, actually gave her life. She was trampled to death when she threw herself in front of King George V's horse as a protest in 1913.

Would I, had I been born earlier, have had the courage to pave the way for change in such a manner? I rather doubt it. Maybe I would have accepted life as it was and suffered the trials of repeated pregnancy and loss, as did my great-grandmother in the 1880s, and coped with a growing family as a full-time housewife without the benefits of today's labour-saving devices. I can't imagine that I would have been happy with such a life but perhaps, if this were the norm and one knew no better, it could be acceptable? In any case, there was probably no choice in those days before the availability of family planning clinics which did not appear until the 1920s, and then in very limited areas and numbers. At least, by the time of my adult life in the 1960s, especially after the introduction of the pill, we had choice. Things have changed dramatically, but even in my lifetime the law against the discrimination of women in the workplace was not actually passed until 1975.

Racial discrimination is still frequently in the news, even though the Race Relations Act was passed in 1976. For me it has never been a problem. People are people, the world over. However, for my mother's generation, although thoughts were more liberal, there was an element of doubt. I remember that at college I made a very good friend, Usha. She was Indian, and as my friend, I naturally invited her home. My parents were happy to entertain her without question. However, when we decided to go across the road for a game of squash, my mother called me to one side with a warning that the club might object to her presence in the club. In fact, there was no problem but 'old fashioned' ideas, although not actually practised at home, were still deeply ingrained in their thinking. One would hope that the younger generations have grown up with other ideas.

Having said this, it is extremely difficult to take on changes and new standards as one gets older. Things learned in childhood often provoke instinctive reactions today. New things can be difficult to learn. It has taken me over thirty years to think in terms of decimal currency, I still have not mastered the art of converting pounds and ounces into grams and kilograms, feet and inches into centimetres and metres, miles into kilometres and feel I never want to understand temperature readings in Centigrade, even though I really do want to know if I am to be hot or cold. How can a government legislate against that? One day, perhaps, I may be sent to prison for requesting a pound of butter because I know, or want to know, no better.

My children now accept the use of the many labour-saving devices that have been introduced since I first married; in fact, not only do they accept them but feel they need to have it all when they first set up home. I don't regret the fact that we started with very little. We learned to be self-sufficient, to entertain ourselves in our free time, to learn how to do the washing, cooking, darning, dressmaking, knitting and housework, literally by hand. No, I would not wish to go back to those days but at least I know I could cope if there was no fast food or ready-made meals, and in any case, I really do prefer home cooking; it is usually cheaper anyway. At least I never had to go back to the days of my mother. The boiler would come out on a Monday morning for the weekly wash which was then put through the mangle, before being put out to dry. Ironing was done with a non-electric flat iron that had to be heated on the stove every few minutes in order to maintain the right temperature. No wonder that she regularly sent shirts and sheets to the laundry. As for refrigeration, there was none; milk was kept cool on a marble slab out of the sun or stood in cold water. The garden runner beans were preserved for consumption in large jars between layers of salt.

We kept fit by walking or cycling to school, and did not know the luxury of being able to jump into the car. Bicycles, buses, trams or trains filled the gap if necessary. We were used to it and it did not create a problem. However, today the thought of life without a car seems like hardship and would grossly restrict involvement in many of the things that make life tick. Yes we have come a long way. Electricity, cars, refrigeration, water in the tap, sewage disposal and all mod cons, we take them all for granted. They make life easier, keep life healthier and give us more free time to enjoy the pleasures of life.

One of the biggest changes in my lifetime has been in the field of communication. My mother remembered the days of the crystal radio that was developed in her early childhood but by the time I arrived, the radio, as we know it, had arrived, but in larger sizes. The few, enormous television sets that first appeared before 1940, signalled a big change in our approach to life, but it was not generally adopted in the home until the early 1950s, at the time of the Coronation of Queen Elizabeth II: and then it was in black and white. It was the advent of colour, which we acquired in the 1960s, that revolutionised the service that so often stops conversation and takes the place of do-it-yourself entertainment. I have had to learn to cope with videos and DVDs but when it comes to iPods, iPhones and computer games, I have to admit it is all too much. However, I have now given in to the computer and email. I now consider them to be essential tools. Thanks to Carol, my daughter and Neil, my son-in-law, who are experts in their use, there is someone to bail me out when things go wrong. I do not know how I would manage without them. Kicking the machine never seems to correct a fault.

We have come a long way from my father's first sighting of an aeroplane in 1913. The skies are full of planes in which one can quickly travel to most parts of the world. Space travel, too, is an actual reality. The first moon landing of humans, in Apollo 11 on 16 July 1969 was a momentous day. Neil Armstrong, Michael Collins and Eugene 'Buzz' Aldrin hit the headlines and were the heroes of the day. Neil Armstrong was the first. His initial words rang round the world clearly: 'One small step for man, one giant leap for mankind'. It was only in 1934 that my grandfather had been amazed at the ability to telephone my father in London. What would he have thought of this message from the moon? The possibility now is of lunar tourism. Voyages to other planets are in the pipeline. One wonders where it will all end.